MANAGING PERFORMANCE

WILEY SERIES IN MANAGEMENT

MANAGING PERFORMANCE

LLOYD BAIRD
School of Management
and
Human Resources Policy Institute
Boston University

John Wiley & Sons
New York Chichester Brisbane Toronto Singapore

Library of Congress Cataloging in Publication Data:

Baird, Lloyd.
Managing performance.

(Wiley series in management)
Includes index.
1. Personnel management. 2. Performance. I. Title.
II. Series.
HF5549.B235 1986 658.3′14 85-3301
ISBN 0-471-06243-X (pbk.)

Printed in the United States of America

10 9 8 7 6 5 4 3 2 1

PREFACE

This book is about two concepts—*performance* and *management*. It is not about objectives, standards, feedback, or appraisals, although these are all important components of performance and are all discussed in the book. The book is about the relationships among these components and the ongoing process of managing performance. Too often, we think of performance management as something that takes place at a point in time, when the objectives are set or when the feedback is given. The focus becomes improving the objectives, adjusting the performance appraisal format and giving good quality feedback—all very important activities but none by themselves manages performance. Performance management is not an event but a process. Performance management is continuous and action oriented with focus on improving performance by using objectives, standards, appraisals, and feedback. The distinction between the two approaches is subtle but critical. If managers are to be successful, their focus must be on improving performance and not on developing and implementing performance management systems. The systems and procedures are the tools—of course they need to be the highest quality possible—but performance is the purpose and that must be the focus of management.

I wrote this book for both managers and students of management. It includes theories and models which explain the concepts and uses cases from organizations to bring them to life. To make the book as useful as possible, I have included questionnaires and tools to apply the concepts and models in organizations. The first chapters in the book explain the concepts and show how to do an organizational analysis to apply them. The book then follows the flow of performance management. However, you need not read it in sequence if your interests and the problems you face seem to relate to one chapter more than others. Read Chapter 1 and then go to the chapter that is the most relevant. If you prefer a different sequence of the chapters, feel free to reorganize them. As with performance management, the importance is not in the sequence or any individual component but how they relate together and how you manage the components simultaneously.

Many people have helped formulate my ideas and provided cases for this book. The original idea came from discussions with W. Clay Hamner and the late Bob St. Clair of St. Clair Press. The ideas began to take root as I worked with organizations developing and implementing performance appraisal systems. I found that the systems, procedures, and training that we developed were much more effective if we took a performance management perspective rather than focusing solely on the appraisals. I am indebted to the organizations that have helped formulate these concepts and brought them to life.

Many colleagues have also helped with the manuscript. Douglas T. Hall is a valued friend, colleague and in this case, editor. He is the master at telling you a manuscript still needs a lot of work and making you feel good about it. Henry Tosi, of the University of Florida, has served as my best critique for this book as with many other projects. He finds holes, inconsistencies, and sloppy thinking in places other people do not even look. Two colleagues I have long worked with in the area of performance management have contributed many thoughts and ideas, Richard Beatty of Rutgers University and Craig Schneier of the University of Maryland. To this list must be added the many reviewers who added their insights to the manuscript. Rick Leyh of John Wiley has been a constant source of exactly the right amount of pressure and support. I, of course, am responsible for the faults and errors in the book.

Three other people deserve credit for making this book possible. My wife, Coleen, supports, prods, and critiques. Never have I seen anyone able to balance so masterfully so many demands and roles as she does. Vince Mahler and Emily Phillip are the magicians at the School of Management Communications Office who turned my writing into typed manuscript. Carla DeFord did a marvelous job of editing. Not only are they technically competent and very productive but they are nice people.

This book is dedicated to managers and students of management. Its purpose is to improve and enhance the most satisfying, involving, and useful of all human behaviors: performance.

Lloyd Baird

CONTENTS

ONE PERFORMANCE AND MANAGEMENT **1**

TWO FITTING THE SITUATION **13**

THREE THE PERFORMANCE AUDIT **23**

FOUR STANDARDS AND MEASURES OF PERFORMANCE **46**

FIVE UNDERSTANDING HUMAN PERFORMANCE **67**

SIX ESTABLISHING AND COMMUNICATING PERFORMANCE EXPECTATIONS **85**

SEVEN SPECIFYING AND MANAGING ACTIVITIES **96**

EIGHT CONTROLLING REWARDS **119**

NINE MANAGING FEEDBACK **137**

TEN MANAGING PERFORMANCE **149**

INDEX **167**

ONE
PERFORMANCE AND MANAGEMENT

This book focuses on two key concepts: performance and management. It provides a framework for analyzing, managing, and improving performance and was written to supplement the study and practice of management. The book's first assumption is that work is purposeful and done to accomplish something. That something may not be immediately obvious or may not appear rational, but it is an integral part of every job. The second assumption is that those desired results should serve as the basis for organizing activities and resources on the job.

As you read this book, you will learn many ways of affecting performance and some reasons for choosing among the alternatives. In order to get started, we begin by defining and explaining the two main concepts and then developing a model for analyzing and managing performance.

PERFORMANCE

As an example of performance, consider the following. Mary supervises 10 employees making electronic components in a plant employing 30 assemblers. The largest component is the size of a television. During a normal month, each employee works on as many as 20 different components. Production is scheduled each week according to the orders received and the workers assigned according to the need. Each worker must know how to assemble each component and have the ability to read engineering drawings explaining how. New products are introduced at the rate of one a month, so workers are constantly learning new assembly procedures. The workers specialize according to what they like to do, some preferring soldering, some are more skilled at assembling small pieces, others more interested in working on the large components. But all workers must be able to shift according to what needs to be done.

Mary has been employed with the firm for 10 years, moving up from production worker to production supervisor, 4 years ago. She is still the most competent assembler and can outproduce anyone she supervises. The group has not changed much over the 4 years Mary has been the supervisor. The organization is good to employees and people do not leave to seek employment elsewhere. When a vacancy exists, it is usually filled by a friend or relative of one of the employees. When the new person joins the group, whoever knows them best takes responsibility for showing them the ropes. The group has production quotas to meet each week and a chart on the rear wall is updated at the end of each day to show how they are doing.

Recently, the firm experienced a tremendous increase in demand for one of the medical products. To meet the demand, 10 more assemblers were hired. Mary's group increased from 10 to 15. Those hired were not experienced and had no natural friends with whom to link up. They reported to work on Monday morning and immediately went to work assembling components. Products were needed quickly and the assumption was that the new employees could learn on the job. The production quotas were increased by 50 percent with the expectation that the long-term employees could take up the slack. Christmas and the holidays were three weeks away and management hoped that all of the commitments made for the product by the end of the year could be met. Employees of the firm had traditionally worked between Christmas and New Year's Day but management decided that as an added incentive, employees would work only until the production quotas had been met. If they finished the monthly quotas before Christmas, they would receive the time between Christmas and New Year's Day off with pay. If they needed a couple of days after Christmas to finish up some left over components, they would work those days and then have the rest off. They would work whatever days needed to complete the production quotas.

The long-term employees set to the task of meeting the production schedule so they could have the week between Christmas and New Year's off. Mary was the most committed because she had relatives visiting. She cut back on the time she spent supervising others and spent her time assembling. She sat at her stool all day assembling, demonstrating she was still the most competent.

At the end of the first week, when only 20 percent of the monthly quota was completed, the group figured they needed to have completed 30 percent to finish up before Christmas. The new employees were obviously not holding up their end of production. Everyone expected them to be a little slower but they were way behind. Mary decided to talk with them as a group and remind them rather strongly that the production group was counting on them.

She called them together 30 minutes before starting time Monday morning of the second week and reminded them of their responsibilities. She explained that they would have to produce twice as much as they did the first week if the group was going to reach its objective. At starting time they seemed to be excited and willing to give it a try, but by the end of the day, production had not improved much for the new group. Mary tried again the next morning calling them together early for a pep talk but again it did not have any effect. Production was still down. By now, the rest of the employees decided that the new employees were not going to be much help and if they were going to meet the quotas, they would have to do it by themselves. Everyone started working harder, hoping to salvage the situation. By the end of the second week, everyone could see that it was hopeless. Discouraged and frustrated, they gave up, production slid below normal level, and this year was like every other year; they worked all of the days between Christmas and New Year's Day.

Performance in this situation, like any other, is a process that unfolds over a period of time. Performance is an action (a verb), not an event (or noun). Performance is action composed of many components, not a result that happens at one point in time. If we are to manage performance, we must manage the action: the verb and not the noun. The outcome (the noun)—the actual result—is what happens because of how we manage the process. Mary, like so many of us, is managing as if performance were an outcome, where all that needs to be done is set the goal and performance happens. Performance management is a continuous process of working with people to accomplish desired results.

As an example of the many components of performance management, again consider Mary. Figure 1-1 shows the components and the relationship among them.

Goals: Performance Expectations

Goals are explanations of desired results: the performance expectations. Implicit in the whole process of performance and management is the desired result. For example, Tosi and Carroll (1982) define management as work that involves the guidance or direction of a group of people toward organizational goals and objectives. Others speak of "getting things done," "accomplishing," and "purposeful behavior." Thus, what differentiates managing activities from mere involvement in those activities is a concern for the results, the sought-after goal. Defined this way, management clearly is not limited to the top of the organization or to any particular job. Subordinates, staff, assistants, spouses, babies, and dogs all manage. They determine what activities to engage in and how to organize those activities to accomplish the outcome they are seeking. In fact, if there is any question about the process of effectively managing desired outcomes, we would do well to observe babies and dogs. Nothing is more effective than the wag-

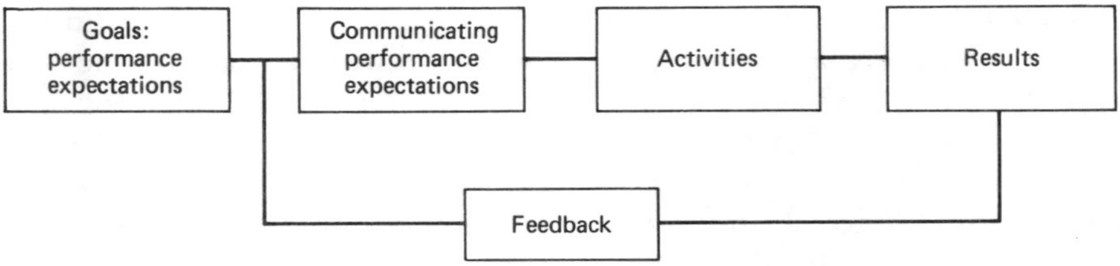

Figure 1-1 The performance process.

ging tail or the crying baby in obtaining desired results. They manage the process; the outcome happens.

Focusing on the desired results sounds simple, but in practice we often become involved in what we are doing and forget why we are doing it. Ordione (1976) refers to this as the activity trap.

> Most managers [and, we would add, people in general] get caught in the Activity Trap! They become so enmeshed in activity, they lose sight of why they are doing it, and the activity becomes a false goal, an end in itself. Falling into the activity trap is not the result of stupidity. In fact, the most intelligent, highly educated people tend to be those most likely to become entrapped in interesting and complex activities. Having spent years mastering one class of activities, they persist in practicing those activities, as learned, even when the objectives practically cry out for some other kind of behavior. The age of specialization has produced a generation of people who have learned to become emotionally attached to irrelevancies. Activity, especially professional activity, often become more and more costly, consuming more and more inputs that are less and less related to any kind of output. . . . As the activity enmeshes a person, he regresses to a more dependent relationship with the input-providers. "You must keep on putting in resources as long as I keep asking for them. But you are not to ask what outputs you are receiving in return." This attitude turns the professionals into the irresponsibles. "I insist that you continue to provide all my needs, without question. As a professional, I am entitled to consume inputs and behave thus."

In Mary's production department, goals for the month were very clear. The goals or performance expectations established what workers were to accomplish, it gave them the target toward which to work. The 15 people who Mary supervised were to produce 400 assembled components.

Communicating Performance Expectations

The first step in translating desired results into actual results is for the worker to understand and accept what must be done. The work environment provides various cues, messages, and indications of what should be accomplished. These messages may be straightforward such as direct requests or they may be subtle hints. In any case, the employee engages in activities based on an understanding and acceptance of the results to be produced.

In Mary's unit, performance expectations were communicated from many sources. A chart on the wall with the goal clearly painted in red provided a visual explanation of the objective and served as a constant reminder. Mary's special meetings and pep talks with the new employees communicated her expectations. Management's promise of days off between Christmas and New Year's Day, the older workers urging of the younger workers, and the reports posted on the graph at the end of the week all communicated performance expectations.

Activities

Once goals have been established and performance expectations communicated, activities, resources, and management practices, etc., must be organized in order to achieve the desired results as efficiently as possible. To accomplish this, the key is to make sure that the goal determines how activities are organized. Too often, we falsely assumed that if a certain set of management principles or rules are followed, employees will be both motivated and productive. The key to successful management is not following fixed principles, but analyzing situations properly and adjusting time and resources to accomplish organizational objectives. Thus, monitoring and analyzing activities in terms of their contribution to organizational objectives becomes critical to good management practices.

Note particularly that many activities and processes must be monitored and analyzed and that both quantitative and qualitative factors should be taken into consideration. Too often, managers focus on the quantitative, that is, on those things that can be easily measured without giving due consideration to less tangible occurrences in the workplace. Activities and processes to be monitored range all the way from the physical handling of a product to the group dynamics and interpersonal relations of employees.

In Mary's group, the activities were the actual day-to-day work of connecting one part with another. Activities also included the daily coffee breaks, the meetings, the informal chatter, and the cleaning of the production area that went on during the day.

Results

Because of the activities of employees, something happens: products are made, relationships among people are created and destroyed, innovations are developed, attitudes are changed, and rewards are received. All may happen simultaneously, making monitoring and analyzing difficult. Even if the goal is unidimensional, the actual results will always be multidimensional. We can't focus only on the physical output in evaluating what happens in a workplace. Work changes people's abilities, expectations, and relationships and also depletes resources. We have to be aware of each of these changes because they affect what can be done in the future.

The most obvious results in the assembly department were the number of completed components at the end of each week. Components were counted as completed products if they passed quality control, so the product results could be described in terms of both quality and quantity. However, other results were also obvious. The animosity between the older employees and the newer employees, the frustration at not having the days off, the lack of cohesiveness in the group, and the strained relationship between Mary and her group were all results of performance.

Feedback

Feedback makes performance dynamic by relating one time period to another. It compares actual results with goals to determine what adjustments are necessary in the activities. Feedback allows management to shift its focus away from activities toward an understanding of the relationships among the goals, environmental cues, employee activities, and actual results obtained on the job. Management becomes a dynamic process of comparing what actually happens to what is supposed to happen and using the difference as a basis for action in the future.

Feedback on Mary's production floor came in many ways. The most obvious was the chart at the end of the room and the production results posted each week. Feedback also happen between people and groups. Informal comments, looks of support or disgust, Mary's meetings with the new employees, management's reports on the production results, and even notes left in production areas by disgruntled employees, notes like "don't destroy Christmas for us" and "Didn't do so well yesterday, did you?"

Together, these components are the performance process. A continuous stream of goals, communication, activities focused on accomplishing desired results and feedback. If performance is a *process of accomplishing desired results,* what is management?

MANAGEMENT

Management is an ongoing dynamic process of helping the desired results to happen. For our purposes, we define management as "the organizing of activities and resources towards desired results." In other words, making sure the work process leads to the desired results in the most efficient way possible. The words in this definition are chosen very carefully. "Organizing" is used instead of coordinating or planning because what is important is not so much what functions managers perform but that they focus on the desired results. "Activities and resources" are used because they are broad enough to include technology, human resources, and information. "Actual results" is used so that we can broaden the normal conception of goals or objectives to include interactions, attitudes, skill development, etc.

The advantage of viewing management in the performance terms of managing activities and resources towards desired results is that the different ways in which managers can affect what is accomplished by the people in the organization is identified (see Figure 1-2). Performance can be managed by the following factors.

1. *Defining the Desired Results (The Goal).* Perhaps the best way to affect accomplishment is to define the desired results (the goal) clearly. Specifying the objectives not only focuses activities in the proper direction, it also energizes those doing the work. With a clear objective, workers see the purpose of their activities and can anticipate the results of them.
2. *Communicating Performance Expectations.* Communicating performance expectations is another common way of affecting what is accomplished. Performance expectations come in a variety of forms: descriptions of the final goal, explanations of what needs to be done, explanations of anticipated results, subtle requests, etc. Controlling communication of performance expectations to affect performance is based on the assumption that if employees know what is expected and understand the situation, they will be better able to accomplish the desired results.
3. *Specifying and Managing the Activities to Be Performed.* The efforts and skills of employees can be focused and directed by the types of activities

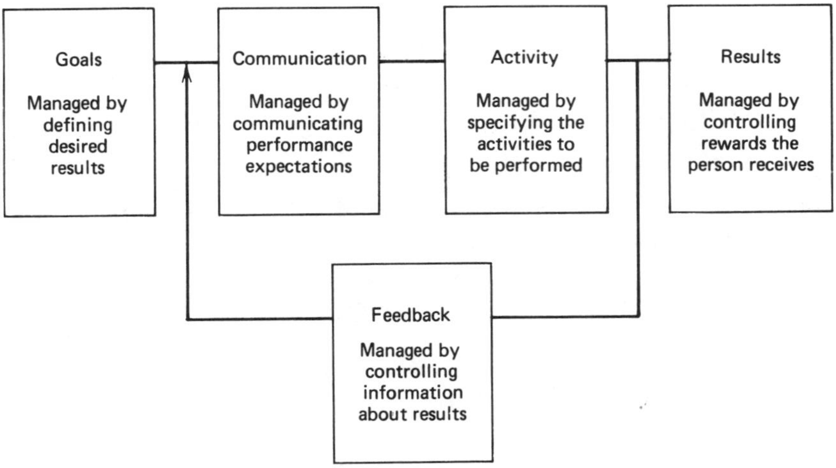

Figure 1-2 Managing the performance process.

they are asked to do. Redefine and manage activities and you will redefine what people are able to accomplish.

4. *Controlling Rewards the Person Receives.* Reward control is a common theme in writings on motivation. The assumption is that individuals desire rewards as personal outcome for activities and gain satisfaction from obtaining them. If rewards are available based on performance, a person gains rewards, hence is satisfied by producing the desired results.
5. *Controlling Information About Results.* The frequency and nature of feedback will have a great affect on what employees do. It provides them with the experience of success or failure and directs their activities.

Performance is managed by managing these components as they support each other, not by managing any one of them separately. Notice particularly how the components relate to one another. Consider the following situation as an example.

A 100-employee firm manufactures garden equipment that ranges from the size of a fertilizer spreader to that of a garden water gauge. The production department consists of 200 employees who assemble by hand the 10 to 50 components that go into each product. They assemble 8000 pieces of equipment during an average month. The sales, however, are increasing so that 10,000 pieces of equipment per month are required. Management decides to see if they can increase productivity to reach the new goal of 1000 components with the same number of employees in the production department. They set the new goal, informed the workers, and began production. At the end of the month, they were disappointed to find that only 7500 pieces had been completed.

The problem in this situation is that the company didn't manage the performance process, they managed only the goal and then waited for results. Instead they should have managed each step of the process by doing the following.

1. Developing an effective way to communicate the new goal.
2. Carefully considering how the work should have been done to meet the goal, designing the jobs so that employees relate to each other properly and are as productive as possible, and assessing their technology and equipment to determine whether changes in that area can improve performance.
3. Constantly monitoring progress to determine how employees are doing and what changes should be made.

At the end of the month, when the goals were not met, management investigated to see what went wrong. They found plenty of parts going into the production system—so many, in fact, that 11,000 pieces of equipment could have been produced. Employees were also well motivated and had time to produce more. Everything was in place to produce 10,000 components a month; it was as if resources were being dumped into a big black hole. Management decided they needed to look at how the work was being done.

They soon found the problem. In the rush to get the product to the customers, Inventory was supplying incomplete kits. Kits were the styrofoam carriers that held all the part of a product. Rather than wait until they had all of the parts, Inventory forwarded the incomplete kit to Production and planned to supply the missing parts when they arrived and as they were needed. Inventory knew that Production had their own private cache of critical spare parts and would be able to supply their own needs assuming they would tell Inventory when more parts were needed.

Production, having used up all their spare parts because of the increased product schedule, took the kits, assembled the product as far as they could, and then set them on the shelves to await new parts. Because no one was managing the total performance process, Inventory never received feedback from Production and never knew what parts were needed. Since there was no feedback mechanism, management never knew what was happening. All they knew was that parts were going into Production and nothing was coming out. They were only managing goals, not performance. Once they looked at the total performance process and began managing all of the components, it became clear that a simple feedback system connecting all of the components in the performance system was needed.

This example is not atypical. Many a Management by Objective (MBO) system fails because managers manage the goals and objectives and nothing else. The activities aren't related to what needs to be accomplished and there is no feedback. MBO becomes an objective-setting system buried in paperwork rather than a management system.

Management by Objectives is not the only management system that runs into trouble because it does not manage the total performance process. Some training programs focus on activities without considering the objectives of the organization, positive reinforcement programs develop elaborate feedback mechanisms that don't relate to organizational goals or help people develop performance skills, performance appraisal systems have no relation to the goals and activities of a job, and job design efforts restructure the activities of jobs without considering the need for feedback mechanisms or performance objectives. Performance management must focus on all the components of performance: goals, communicating performance expectations, activities, actual results, and feedback. All components must be managed together to create an integrated performance management system, and everyone is responsible for managing them.

THE DYNAMIC NATURE OF PERFORMANCE MANAGEMENT

Because performance is a process, managing performance is dynamic and involves time as one of the key elements that must be managed. One way in which time becomes part of performance management is the sequence of events. Some events happen before others. For example goals should be set and performance expectations communicated before feedback comparing results and goals is given. Also because some events happen before others, some components are more directly linked to the final results than others. Activities directly affect results, while feedback has to be used to compare the desired results with the actual and then translated into activity before it affects final results.

In a situation such as Mary's, where the desired result is clearly defined for everyone, activities determine what is accomplished. Logically, in this situation, the first component Mary should manage is employee activities. Once the employees have been trained how to do the job, attention can be turned to feedback and rewards. Mary will accomplish little by giving assemblers negative feedback and pressure to perform jobs they do not know how to do. This is the wrong focus for performance management. Depending on the situation, some components of performance management are more important than others and some components are more directly related to results. What you focus on in any situation should be determined by what will have the most direct and lasting effect on performance.

Another way time becomes part of performance management is through lags. Changes do not immediately have an effect. For example, assume that sales are low in a sales force you supervise. You decide something has to be done quickly. The nature of the job can't be changed much, so you decide to change the monetary rewards and see if that helps. Up until now, the sales force has been on straight salary. You have been reading about positive reinforcement programs and decide to put them on an incentive system. You wait a week and nothing happens. The sales force understands the new system well enough, but they aren't selling any more products. You wait another week, and still nothing happens. Two months later you finally give up and decide to go back to the salary system, only this time you decide that the central office will coordinate sales calls to get a little tighter control of what is happening. The sales force will be dispatched from the central office and asked to report back on the results. All present customers will go into a central pool and the central office will control all assignments.

Now consider what was probably happening. The good performers were excited with the new incentive system and did the background work necessary to develop long-term clients. Just about when they had their customers on board, they received the memo saying all clients will be transferred into a central pool and assigned by central administration. The most productive workers will become the most dissatisfied as a result of this change. If you knew how long the sales force takes to adapt to a new system, these problems could probably have been avoided. You were reacting to information about past performance, not the future.

In summary, viewing performance as a process that includes time has three implications for management.

1. Some components of the performance process happen before others and the sequence is important. You cannot manage activities before you know what is to be accomplished. You cannot give feedback before something is done.
2. Some components are closer to results than others. Activities directly affect results. Feedback, however, must be communicated and then translated into activities before it affects results.
3. There will be lags that are likely to occur between the implementation of changes in any of the components of the performance process and their effect on results.

SUMMARY

This chapter has presented the theory of performance that will serve as the basis for chapters to follow. Performance is a process that leads to results. Managing is the organizing of activities and resources toward those results. Actual results can be affected by changing any of the components in the process, goals, communications, activities, or feedback. The challenge in improving performance is to decide how each of the components of performance process should be managed. All of the components must be in place. The dynamic nature of performance requires that not only must you manage all the components to affect present performance but you must realize how they will affect future performance.

In the remainder of this book we consider the techniques you can use to manage performance. First, we review how to fit performance management to the situation. Then, we discuss three general competencies you will need to manage performance.

Chapter 2	How to fit performance management to the situation.
Chapter 3	How to conduct a performance audit to determine how technology, structure and human resources fit together providing the opportunities and constraints within which performance is managed.
Chapter 4	How to measure performance so that it can be analyzed and managed.
Chapter 5	How to understand human behavior and motivation.

The next four chapters look at each of the components of performance and how they are managed.

Chapter 6 Establishing and communicating performance expectations.
Chapter 7 Specifying and managing activities.
Chapter 8 Controlling rewards.
Chapter 9 Managing feedback.

The last chapter provides an overview integrating all we have covered.

Chapter 10 Performance management.

TWO
FITTING THE SITUATION

We have identified many ways of affecting what is accomplished: defining the desired results, communicating performance expectations, specifying and managing activities, controlling rewards, and controlling information. Which one should you use? Should you use all of them? The appropriate strategy for managing performance is to spend time and energy where it will contribute most to producing the desired result. You must fit the situation. Two factors will influence what components of the performance process you should focus on: the competence of the employee and the complexity of the job to be done. Consider each factor separately and then combine them to describe the various types of management situations.

COMPETENCE OF THE INDIVIDUAL

The first factor to consider when determining how to manage performance is the competence of the employee. Workers who are learning how to do a job need different management support and attention than those who already know how and have the skills to be good performers. Before discussing that statement, let us make sure the definitions are clear. For those who already know how to perform, their dominant responses are correct. When acting spontaneously, they will do their job correctly and accomplish good results by devoting the right amount of effort. They know what needs to be done and how to do it, the question is doing it. When people are learning, their dominant responses are incorrect; that is, they cannot spontaneously do their job correctly. They have to acquire new skills and knowledge. When people are learning, they can achieve good results only by changing or improving themselves. No amount of time and energy devoted to doing the wrong things will achieve the desired results. They don't know what needs to be done or how to do it.

Note that our definition of learning is somewhat different than psychological reinforcement theory. Reinforcement theories are concerned with people exhibiting correct responses. Persons who know how to do what is required may choose not to, because they have not been rewarded in the past. When they are rewarded, however, they will presumably engage in the appropriate behavior and, thus, be considered to have "learned" the correct response. Our definition of learning assumes that a person does not know how to do what is required and must develop the ability to respond correctly.

Managers should focus on different parts of the performance process when dealing with people who are learning as opposed to those who already know for two reasons. First, people need different types of information in each situation. When learning, people need information about what is to be accomplished and how it is to be done. They need help in understanding what resources are available to them (e.g., time, skills, materials, technology, etc.) and how they should be used. Once people have had a chance to try a job, they need to know what they did right or wrong. They need to understand how what they did led to the results and what needs to be changed in order to achieve the desired results. When people are learning, both employees and their managers need to focus on the first components of performance: desired results, activities, and the resources and skills to do them properly. When people know how to do the job they need feedback on results. They need to know what they have accomplished, then the focus shifts to outcomes.

A second consideration in dealing with inexperienced employees is their level of arousal or energy. Research has found that when people are excessively aroused, they will do what they already know. When people are under pressure, they don't have time to think or reflect on their actions, they cannot learn new ways of acting. All they can do is respond. Not all arousal is bad, however; people must be excited enough to keep focused on the work at hand. The point is that when learning, the appropriate level of arousal is lower than when we are performing a job we know well.

Competition is one common cause of excessive arousal. The pressure to do well often causes us to get so excited we can't pay attention to what we are doing and learn from our mistakes. Instead of improving performance, the pressure of competition will actually worsen it if we are not aware of what we are doing and don't have time to reflect and learn. In this case, the pressure of competition will often lead to frustration. Excessive arousal can also be caused by working in groups or for audiences that expect a high level of performance before we have learned our job. In these cases, we not only have the pressure generated by our own desire to perform well, but we have group pressures. If we are learning a job and are expected to perform it expertly at the same time, the resulting pressure can cause mistakes and anxiety that may worsen our performance.

In summary, because of the effect of arousal and the needs of the person who is learning, management should be oriented differently in learning and performance situations. In learning situations, people need assistance in developing skills and learning how to use them; they need to know what resources are available, and how to change what they are doing. In this case, management should focus on helping people understand the goals and activities of the job and develop the right skills, without demanding a high level of performance too quickly.

In a performance situation (where the dominant response is correct), management should concern itself with communicating performance expectations and letting employees know how far from the desired result they are. Presumably, the employees will know what to do once they find this out. They need only devote sufficient enough energy to the job to accomplish their goals. Management systems that focus on results can provide the experienced worker with the information and arousal necessary for him or her to do the job well.

The general rule is, then, the more competent the person, the more management should focus on actual results. The less competent the worker, the more you should focus on how the work is done.

NATURE OF THE TASK

The second factor to consider in determining how to manage performance is the complexity of the task itself. A task may be complex in several ways: first, many activities may be happening at once. In this case, resources and skills must be juggled to produce the desired results. When multiple inputs and multiple results exist, there will also be constant questions about the relationship between what needs to be accomplished and the available resources: How should these skills, efforts, and resources be combined? Which results have priority? Which will contribute most to the desired results?

The more diverse the desired results, the more performers will have to balance their time and resources. Consider for example, a teacher. Teachers have limited time and resources to devote to their students, and each student will have different needs. Although some techniques expand the teacher's limited resources, beyond a certain point, time spent with one student has to be taken away from the others or from the class as a whole. Time and energy must be balanced in order to achieve the best results with the highest number of students.

In this situation, the teacher must pay attention to the relationship among all the elements contributing to effective teaching. The teacher must understand not only the multiple inputs of performance, but how they are transformed into the desired result, the teacher must focus on the process involved in achieving desired results.

Tasks may be complex not only because they have many inputs and results, but also by virtue of their unpredictability. Relationships among the components of performance may be uncertain and changing, the desired results may not be clearly defined, the availability of resources may be uncertain, or there may not be a clear understanding of what resource or skills are necessary. In these cases, predicting the outcome of one's actions is difficult; results will be hard to understand, let alone control. This unpredictability will again make focusing on inputs and activities important so that the relationships among the resources, skills, etc. can be managed as well as possible.

A political candidate or officeholder is a good example of someone managing a complex situation. The final goal is often clear—winning the election or passing the bill—but the way to reach it may be very uncertain. Good performance will be determined by how accurately the environment can be monitored and how quickly changes can be made. Because monitoring changes and adapting to them is so critical to the politician, these ought to be his or her focus. Attention must be given to the initial phases of performance; goals, resources, skills, and activities. A competent politician must conduct numerous voter surveys, hold endless staff meetings, negotiate and compromise, participate in ceremonies, give speeches, etc. All necessary so that the politician can effectively manage activities and be prepared to adjust to environmental changes.

In a complex situation, performance is maintained and improved by making sure the right information is available. A relentless and limited focus on one aspect of the campaign will be counterproductive. All individuals who are involved in obtaining the desired result must focus on how the desired result is to be obtained and be willing to shift strategy when necessary.

The general rule then is, the *more* complex the task, the *more* management should focus on the initial phases of performance. The simpler the task, the more attention should be given to the final results.

The complexity of the task and the competence of the people involved can be combined to develop a model for identifying which components of performance deserve the closest attention in various situations. Consider several situations (see Figure 2-1).

SITUATION 1: LEARNING A SIMPLE TASK

When learning a simple task, an employee will not yet know what to do or how to do it. He or she must learn the correct responses. In a simple task, few skills and resources are necessary. These skills and resources have a predictable relationship with the few desired results. One caution to remember, referring to a task as simple does not mean it is easy or unimportant.

Complexity of the Task	Low Competency of the Person	High Competency of the Person
High	Low Pressure for Results Help worker learn how to monitor environment and choose and develop proper skills	Moderate Pressure for Results Provide information about environment Help worker remember and understand past experiences Help worker understand activities
Low	Low Pressure for Results Focus on feedback and information to facilitate learning Help employee learn proper activities	High Pressure for Results Goals and activities understood; little time is spent on them

Figure 2-1 Managing performance in different situations.

Often the tasks with few inputs and outputs and predictable relationships are hard to do and the most important. For example, without the bookkeeper the bank does not work.

Before the individual attempts the simple task, management should explain what is expected, what resources are available, and how the resources should be used (i.e., the desired results, resources, and activities involved). After the individual has performed the task several times, managements' and employees' attention should be shifted to the skills and resources used, how they were used, and the results they produced. Workers need information and help analyzing what they have done and learning from their mistakes. Without the proper assistance, they are left on their own to guess what went wrong and how to make improvements.

When the worker is learning, strong emphasis on actual results is not advisable. Pressure to produce coming from constant attention to results would probably lead to excessive arousal, causing the individual to be less attentive to the skills and activities to be learned. Actual results shouldn't be totally ignored, however; they provide the necessary gauge of how well skills are being learned.

A new employee on an assembly line who is assigned a repetitive, predictable job is learning a simple task. The desired results are few and concrete enough to be explained easily; the necessary skills and how they should be used are predictable. As the employee begins the job, the manager should explain what is expected of him or her and help the employee to develop and use the proper skills. As these skills are learned, the manager's time and attention can be shifted away from helping the employee learn skills to applying more pressure for results.

Many jobs would fall into this category. Consider a dental hygienist, for example. Certain skills are necessary to do the job, and once they are learned, the situation doesn't change much. Consider also some jobs in bookkeeping, banking, inventory, or certain personnel fuctions. To a certain extent, what makes these jobs so valuable is their predictability and simplicity. Basic banking systems have to be simple enough for a large number of people to understand them and they have to be used the same way by everyone or they won't work. Every teller can't use different procedures, forms, and methods because the results have to be predictable and unchangeable. At the end of the day, the books must be balanced, and certain procedures are necessary for that to be accomplished.

The same applies to the bookkeeper, the wage and salary clerk, the inventory control specialist, etc. The jobs may be simple in the sense of having few predictable inputs and results but they still have to be learned, and learning them requires an understanding of what the desired results are and how the results can be accomplished.

SITUATION 2: PERFORMING A SIMPLE TASK

When a person is performing a simple task, the correct responses have already been acquired. Remember a simple task has (1) few desired results and (2) what needs to be done in order to produce the desired results is highly predictable. Once the worker has learned all the necessary skills, the problem for the manager is to keep motivation high and properly directed by focusing on results. Doing well does not depend on acquiring new skills, but on devoting enough time and energy to the job. Management must develop systems keeping employees focused on the desired results, and then evaluate what is actually accomplished in relations to the goal.

The tasks in this situation are the same ones identified in situation 1, but here the person has learned the proper responses. As in the case of the bookkeeper, bank teller, or dental hygienist, once a person has learned the skills necessary to accomplish a simple task, the challenge is to motivate them to do it. This can best be done by focusing on the desired results and comparing them to what is actually accomplished.

SITUATION 3: LEARNING A COMPLEX TASK

Complex tasks demand multiple resources and skills, have many desired results, and have unclear, unpredictable relationships between inputs and results. Hence, some of the skills necessary for performing these tasks focus on monitoring and interpreting an unpredictable environment. Workers must learn to understand the relationships between resources, skills, and results as best they can. They need to develop a range of skills necessary for many different situations. Most of all, they must learn how to change and develop as the situation changes.

People in this type of situation need to learn and understand the following factors.

1. The multiple, changeable, and unpredictable nature of the goals toward which they will be working.
2. The many resources, skills, and practices necessary to perform the task. Because many combinations of these factors are possible, the employee must also learn how to select from among the alternatives.
3. Monitoring the environment. Because of the many inputs and outputs and the unpredictable nature of the environment in which the worker must function, important skills will be monitoring what is happening and adapting to the changing situation.
4. The activities that will most probably lead to the desired results. Because many results are desired, many activities are important. Not only must workers learn each activity, they must develop an appreciation of when to engage in each one.
5. The actual results. Understanding what has been accomplished provides a gauge for adjustments and will help the worker gain an appreciation of multiple goals. Too much emphasis on actual results will, however, lead to undesirably high levels of arousal and frustration, and these may impede the learning process.

Many jobs involve complex tasks. Medicine, administration, sales, electronics, research and development, etc. all have multiple inputs and outputs with unpredictable relationships among them. Most managers also have complex jobs in which they must learn many skills and be able to employ a wide range of responses to the situations with which they are confronted.

The nature of a complex job suggests some of the ways a manager can help an employee learn the job, as shown in the following list.

1. The manager can provide information about job activities. While the activities involved in a simple job do not change, the opposite is true of complex jobs—what is appropriate now may not be appropriate in the future. Therefore, the manager needs to pay attention not only to what is being done at present but also to other activities that may become important in the future as the situation changes.
2. Because the task involved in the job is unpredictable and changeable, the worker will need to develop the ability to monitor the situation and adjust his or her behavior. Management can help the worker focus not only on the present but also the future.
3. Management should lessen the emphasis on results (1) because the person needs to concentrate on learning the correct skills and responses

and (2) because the environment is so complex sustained emphasis on results might create the illusion that the job is more consistent and stable than it really is. The worker needs help in understanding what the relationships are between what they do on the job and what they accomplish. There should be only enough focus to reinforce their importance and give the worker an appreciation of what is to be learned.

SITUATION 4: PERFORMING A COMPLEX TASK

When a person knows how to perform a complex task, management can facilitate performance by doing the following.

1. Provide workers with necessary information to analyze the situation properly and monitor changes in their goals and constraints within which they operate.
2. Help workers remember and understand past experiences. In a complex task so much happens at once that workers will not be able to remember all the relevant facts about what has happened on their own. Management should help them collect, store, and summarize information about their experiences.
3. The performance process takes activities and transforms them into accomplishments. When few predictable inputs and results exist, this transformation process is easy to understand. When multiple inputs and outputs and unclear relationships between them exist, the ways that input transformed into the results will not be as clear. Management will need to help workers understand how their skills and the resources can fit together to produce the desired results.

When experienced employees are performing complex tasks, management should develop systems focusing on all stages of the performance process. Management's main concern should be to provide the performer with the information and support necessary to analyze the situation as accurately as possible and then act in accordance with his or her analysis to produce the desired result.

Two main differences between performing a complex task and the other three situations we have reviewed are important to note. First, so much happens in the workplace and so much is unpredictable that management can't assume performers will remember and collect all the information they need to make the right decisions. Management must help them. Second, management must not focus solely on desired results and expect the worker to be able to make everything fall into place. Complex tasks are just too unpredictable. The performer needs help monitoring and diagnosing the situation.

In most complex tasks, the performer is always learning because the situation is always changing. In some complex situations, the people involved have nearly all the requisite skills and abilities. For instance, let us extend our previous example and consider the work of a very competent politician. The number of results are limited only by his or her imagination. The resources to accomplish them are varied and scattered. The politician has to assemble and digest vast quantities of information and monitor voter preferences as well as what is happening in the legislature. Because of experience and ability, however, the seasoned politician will generally know what to do after acquiring the necessary information.

The politician will also provide us with an illustration of why management practices and systems can't focus solely on outcomes in complex tasks. Because the legislature is a forum for negotiation and compromise, the final form of a law will often be very different from that of the original bill. For the politician, the final law may not be exactly what was desired when he or she introduced the bill, but the relationships and resources acquired along the way will be valuable in the future.

In the political arena, not paying attention to the relationships formed in the process of doing legislative work would be folly. If the total focus was on specific results, bills would never pass the legislature because sponsors wouldn't be willing to compromise. The best chance the politician has to affect results is to very carefully manage the process.

Another example of a complex task that demonstrates the importance of understanding the total performance process is the work of a courtroom attorney. The general goal of the attorney is to win the case, but the specific actions necessary to manage the case are fairly unpredictable. They will remain ambiguous until the lawyer enters the courtroom and discovers the opponent's strategy. In preparing for a case, the lawyer must focus on preparing briefs, planning defenses, lining up witnesses, etc. The focus will be on resources, skills, and activities. Having entered the courtroom, the lawyer can shift attention to the final objective of winning the case. As the trial progresses, which portions of the preparation to use will become clearer; however, the lawyer must still continue to assess what actions to take and how best to take them. The lawyer cannot focus solely on the ultimate goals of winning the case but must manage the process of doing so. Complex tasks require that the performer focus on all the stages of the performance process in turn.

SUMMARY

Working at the individual level, certain components need more attention than others. The more competent the employee, the more management practices and systems should focus on actual results. The less competent the worker, the more management practices and systems should focus on how the work is done, that is, the process of obtaining the desired result. The more complex the task, the more the manager and the worker should focus on the initial phases of performance. The simpler the task, the more pressure and attention should be given to final results.

Managing performance is not a set of rules to follow. Managing performance is understanding the performance process, analyzing the situation, and fitting the process to the situation.

THREE
THE PERFORMANCE AUDIT

Before we consider the specific techniques for managing each component of performance, we need to set the stage by talking about the general organizational context within which performance is managed. This context is a combination of human resources, technology, and organizational structure. To begin, we need to distinguish between human performance and organizational performance. Human performance is that portion of the results that can be attributed to people in the organization and is the focus of this book. Organizational performance is the total final result that is determined by the combination of human resources, technology, and organizational structure (see Figure 3-1). Human performance is managed within the context set by technology and organizational structure. Human and organizational performance may not be the same. On the production line, the final results are greatly determined by the technology and resources used. Great improvements in skills, abilities, and effort by line employees (human performance) might not have much affect on the actual results (organizational performance) because they are constrained by the technology and resources with which they work. Big changes in organizational performance will come when the technology and resources are changed. Similarly, changes in technology and resources might not have much effect on organizational performance in an advertising agency. As one chief executive of a large advertising agency recently said, "Our assets go down in the elevator every night." Big changes in organizational performance will result when employees improve their performance.

In this chapter, we discuss each contextual factor, consider their relative contribution to organizational performance, and suggest a performance audit for determining how they relate together. By understanding the context established by the technology and structure, you will be much more able to manage human performance. Figure 3-2 presents the performance audit used to analyze organizational performance.

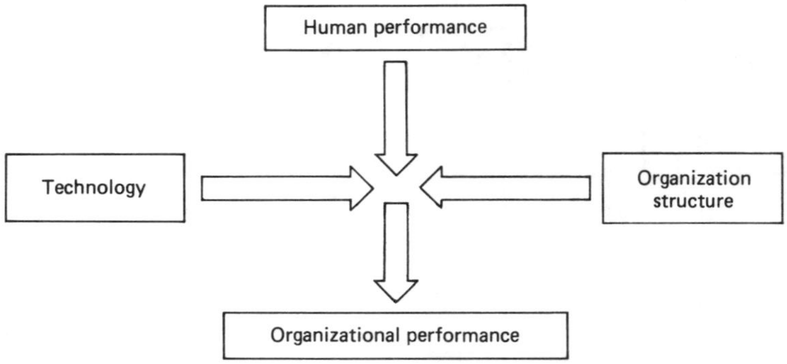

Figure 3-1 Human and organizational performance.

THE THREE FACTORS OF ORGANIZATIONAL PERFORMANCE

The three factors of organizational performance, technology, structure, and human resources, are present in every organization. In an assembly line sophisticated technology may dominate the work but the worker is still a contributing factor. In writing a book the author is the most important factor, but the typewriter or word processor, and paper still make a contribution. Consider the nature of each component.

Technology and Materials

Every job has materials and technology. Materials are the physical resources and technology is the equipment, machinery, and tools used in production. The technology of a steel mill would be the furnaces and inventory systems, the materials would be iron ore and office supplies. For an advertising firm, technology would include computers, media, and air transportation, and materials would be the paint, paper, and supplies used in advertising.

Technology is a critical factor in organizational performance and must be conscientiously managed. No amount of human effort can compensate for hopelessly outdated technology. The older manufacturing facilities of the Northeast, for instance, are much less efficient than the modern plants being built in the South and that will have a negative effect on organizational performance in the Northeast. Fast-growing industries such as electronics, aviation, and plastics contantly develop new products and better ways of manufacturing. In these industries, technology is critical and must be constantly managed. Often the productivity of an organization will be determined by its technology.

Structure

Organizational structure includes two aspects of organizations. First, what is included in the job? What are the responsibilities and activities of the job? What are the rules and regulations governing it? How is the job supposed to be done? What are the goals, the desired results? Second, what are the relationships that exist among jobs? Organizations are sets of interdependent activities. Not only does each person have a defined job to do but that job must fit with other jobs in some meaningful way. It does no good to have various units generating products that cannot be related to the overall organizational goals.

As an example of the way organizational structure affects what can be accomplished, consider a hospital. Many types of jobs are involved: doctors, nurses, technical workers, administration, etc. What is included in each job and the way the jobs relate to each other together will have an effect on what is accomplished. One way to structure a hospital is to centralize authority and responsibility with the doctors making all decisions and nurses and technical support serving as staff to carry them out. If doctors are the experts and are always available, performance will be good. But if no doctors are available or if emergencies arise where there is no time to consult doctors, or if the problem is nonmedical and doctors have no expertise to bring to the situation, performance will be poor.

A decentralized structure where nurses and support staff are allowed to make decisions they are qualified to make usually results in a more productive hospital. All of the decisions in a hospital are not medical decisions and they don't need to be made by doctors; forms need to be filled out, budgets balanced, waste disposed of, and analyses of efficiency completed. In nonmedical areas such as these, persons other than doctors are perfectly capable of making decisions.

Human Resources

People bring all of their characteristics, skills, abilities, and attitudes to their jobs often making human resources the hardest factor of organizational performance to manage. Unlike technology, which once in place, works the same way until altered, people change. They learn, they grow, and their attitudes change over time. They don't always work in the same way and they all can't be managed in the same way.

With human resources, the substantial variations among people must be anticipated and managed. Ongoing analysis of the status of the firm's human resources must be conducted and human resources management practices continuously updated.

The Performance Audit

I. What are the relative contributions of the various factors of performance?

A. Technology

1. How much capital investment is needed to create and sustain the workers' jobs?

2. How dynamic is the technology (i.e., how long does it take for new technology to become obsolete)?

3. To what extent can a competitive advantage be gained by using technically superior methods?

4. If financial conditions make it impossible to invest money in technology in the future, would productivity eventually start to decrease? If so, how much would it decrease and how fast?

B. Structure

1. What proportion (how much) of the inputs are needed from other units or people in order to achieve good performance?

Figure 3-2 The performance audit.

2. How many other people or units use the outputs of the job?

3. How critical (how important) are the various inputs received from the outside? Is performance dependent on them?

4. Is performance dependent on those who absorb the outputs?

5. How much discretion does the person doing the job have in controlling:
   a. Resources and other performance input?

   b. The market where the product is distributed?

6. How many resources suppliers are there? How many outlets are there for the products of the employee's performance?

C. Human Resources
   1. Is increased effort likely to lead to increased productivity?

Figure 3-2 (*Continued*)

2. How much skill is involved in the task? Does it really make a difference whether you have the right people on the job?

II. Which components are presently limiting performance?

1. Where is the idle capacity and slack? Are technology and materials being used to capacity? Are employees devoting all their skills and energy to the job?

2. If the technology were upgraded, would there be unused human potential? Would workers have to be retrained?

3. Could the organizational structure be changed to increase performance of the present technology?

4. Are the individuals in the organization grouped in the most productive way possible? Could they be rearranged without changing the technology?

Figure 3-2 (*Continued*)

5. Are employees working as effectively as they can? If employees skills and efforts were improved, would performance improve?

III. Which factor do you have enough control over in the short and long term that you can change it to improve performance?

1. What can be changed on the job without approval from superiors?

2. What can the superiors approve without checking with others? What are they most likely to approve?

3. How long would it take to make effective changes in each of the factors?

4. How long would it be before the changes had an effect on performance?

5. Must subordinates accept a change before it will be effective? If so, how is this acceptance gained?

Figure 3-2 (*Continued*)

THE PERFORMANCE AUDIT

The purpose of the performance audit is to investigate how the three factors—technology, organizational structure, and human resources—relate to each other and to organizational performance. The audit is done on the assumption that the relative importance and the degree of control management has of the factors must be considered in deciding how to manage human performance. The most important components should receive the most attention, but often the most important are not controllable. So you recognize the constraints under which you operate and focus on the most important component you control.

A performance audit consists of three questions.

1. What are the relative contributions (importance) of the various components to this organization's performance?
2. Which components are presently limiting performance?
3. Which component(s) do you control enough in the short and long term to make changes?

What Are the Relative Contributions (Importance) of the Various Components of Performance?

A good way to conceptualize this first step in the performance audit is to think about constraints on performance. For purposes of illustration, assume that the organization under study mass produces stoneware for use in the kitchen. The organization uses an assembly-line process in which the employees are responsible for quality control at each stage of manufacturing. With this particular product, the technology involved is probably the most important factor of the organization's performance. By important, we mean that it has the greatest impact on what can be accomplished. A certain amount of time, effort, and money spent on technology will have more of an effect on the final outcome than the same amount spent on organizational structure or human resources. Following are examples of situations where the importance of the contextual factors to organizational performance varies.

Mass production is typical of one type of work where vast amounts of technology are necessary. As long as the assembly line dominates the performance process, the levels and types of performance will be determined largely by the characteristics of the technology. Human resources are undoubtedly important, but their main function is to complement the technology. Obtaining skilled, motivated employees to work on the assembly line will probably not affect performance as much as changing the assembly line itself.

Structure is more important than the other factors of organizational performance in work where jobs must be well integrated in order to work toward common objectives. Task forces or research and development units are examples of jobs in which the ways people work together will often determine what is accomplished. In research and development work, technology plays a critical role, but ultimately productivity will be determined by how well the researchers can work together to solve problems. Researchers are often so specialized that they cannot solve certain problems by themselves. Each specialist will have a piece of information that must be fitted with other pieces to discover the final solution. If the pieces don't fit together properly, nothing will be accomplished. The specialists have to work together, and the structure determines how.

Human resources are most important in labor intensive organizations where the basis of the work is people's skill and energy. Most service industries are labor intensive—consider the hair stylist or the barber. Technological changes do occur in these fields; for instance blow driers, vibrating machines, vacuum cleaners, new combs, etc.; but the most important factor in the final product has always been, and will probably always be, the skill of the barber. Human resources is the most important factor in organizational performance.

Now that we have briefly introduced each of the factors, consider how they relate to and affect each other. Each component has characteristics that indicate how significant it is for organizational performance.

Technology The way to determine the importance of technology is to determine how much money the firm has invested in it and how fast it changes. Technology and materials come in the form of fixed assets and tangible resources. The larger the investment in technology, the more unable and/or unwilling the organization will be to make changes because of the great cost involved. Also, the greater the investment in technology, the more centralized the decisions regarding the investment will be. People lower in the hierarchy won't have control over the technology they use; it is simply a constraint within which the employee must operate. For example, eliminating or changing the assembly line at a manufacturing plant would not be an alternative available to middle-level management.

In addition to size of investment, rate of change is another characteristic determining how important technology is to performance. Each organization has a unique technology that becomes obsolete at a certain rate and must be replaced by a superior method in order to remain competitive. Sometimes the technology wears out and needs replacing; at other times it just becomes obsolete. In situations where the technology changes quickly, organizations will gradually fail if they don't adapt (this has been particularly true of electronic firms recently). Thus, rate of change is another good indicator of how much attention should be given to technology.

The organizations in which technology is most critical is where both conditions exist simultaneously: a large investment in technology that is rapidly changing. For example, in large organizations producing computers, electronic equipment, or sophisticated aviation and military equipment. it is obvious that technology must be consciously managed if the organizations are to survive.

The following questions are useful for evaluating the importance of technology to performance.

1. How much capital investment is needed to create and sustain the workers' jobs?
2. How dynamic is the technology, that is, how long does it take for new technology to become obsolete?
3. To what extent can a competitive advantage be gained by using technically superior methods?
4. If financial conditions make it impossible to invest money in technology in the future, would productivity eventually begin to decrease? If so, how much would it decrease and how fast?

Structure We have defined organizational structure as the activities and responsibilities included in any job and the relationships among the jobs in the organization. In general, the more dependent a person is on others to do his or her job, the more important the organizational structure becomes. If a market researcher depends on data, materials, computer analyses, and the like from others, he or she better have good working relationships with the people who provide those resources.

The best way to analyze dependence is in terms of resource control: How much do others control the resources you need? If a resource is critical to one's performance, those who control it wield a great deal of power, and the relationship with them deserves close attention.

Pfeffer and Salancik (1978) suggest two ways of determining the importance of relationships with others. One is to analyze what percentage of the resources necessary to successfully perform the job comes from other people? For example, does all of the necessary market information come from others or can the market researcher generate his or her own? The second is to analyze the importance of the resources received from others? Could the person continue to function without the resource? For example, others may provide only a limited amount of information to the market researcher but that information might be so important that no analysis can be done without it.

In addition to being dependent on others for information and resources, we can be dependent on them to absorb our output. For example, consider a staff unit that does legal analysis for the president's office of an organization. They only work for this one unit and are totally dependent on it. No one else can use what they produce. In this case, the structure of the firm must be such that the legal staff has a good working relationship with the staff of the president's office.

The following questions will help you analyze the importance of organizational structure to a person or unit.

1. What proportion (how much) of the inputs are needed from other units or people in order to achieve good performance?
2. How many other people or units use the outputs of the job?
3. How critical (how important) are the various inputs received from the outside? Is performance dependent on them?
4. Is performance dependent on those who absorb the outputs?

Another characteristic of dependence that Pfeffer and Salancik (1978) propose is "discretion over resource allocation and use." How much control do individuals have over the resources? If they have a great deal of control, their dependency on other people is reduced even though the resource itself might be critical to their job. If you have your own electric power generator you will not be dependent on others for power to run your computer. This same concept applies to production. One way to gain control is to become a sole supplier or market. If you can only get electricity from one source, that source has a great deal of control over what you can do. As J. D. Thompson (1967) notes, "an individual's dependence on others is inversely related to the ability of the individual to obtain resource inputs from alternative sources."

These concepts suggest two more questions that can be used to investigate the importance of one's relationship to others (i.e., the importance of organizational structure).

5. How much discretion does the person doing the job have in controlling resources, and other performance input and the market where the product is distributed?
6. How many resource suppliers are there? How many outlets are there for the products of the employee's performance?

In summary, as these questions suggest, having the right organizational structure is important when the input obtained from others and the sources to which the employee's output goes are (1) necessary for organizational performance, (2) not controlled by the employee on the job, and (3) limited to a few sources.

Human Resources The importance of human resources is determined by the skill and effort required in the production process. Some situations exist in which increasing skill and effort will make little difference in results. For example, increasing the skill of individuals on an assembly line without comparable changes in technology is not likely to have much of an effect.

In some jobs, however, skill and effort make substantial contributions to productivity. Teachers, dentists, and lawyers all rely heavily on their skills to do their jobs. Two questions should help you analyze the importance of human resources to organizational productivity.

1. Is increased effort likely to lead to increased productivity?
2. How much skill is involved in the task? Does it really make much difference to have the right type of people on the job?

Which Components Are Limiting Performance?

Once the major contributors to performance are determined, it would seem that all that is needed is to improve them. If certain materials and technology are the most important factors in the production of minicomputers, then performance will improve if we obtain more of these materials and better technology, right? Wrong; improving performance is not that simple in most organizations because all of the factors or organizational performance are interrelated.

Even though technology may be the most important component in the firm that produces minicomputers, other factors may be limiting performance. More technology may be available than the employees know how to handle. In that case, even if more resources and better technology were obtained, the employees wouldn't have the time, energy, and skill necessary to use it. Human resources then constrain the firm's performance.

The factor of organizational performance to focus on at any particular time is the one limiting performance. Notice particularly this may not be the most important factor. In the stoneware manufacturer example, technology was more important than human resources. If the necessary technology is available but not enough operators are working, and those working are improperly trained, then human resources will be the limiting factor in the firm's performance. Improving and increasing technology will not help if their usefulness is being constrained by the employees. The manager must address the human resources problems in order to improve organizational performance.

Human resources commonly constrain performance when new technology is adopted. For example, when a new hospital is built with all of the most modern equipment, when a new packaging process is introduced in a manufacturing plant, or when personnel records in an organization are computerized, performance often deteriorates. The employees may rebel and refuse to occupy the hospital, or they may be unwilling to use the new packaging equipment or the computer. In these situations, technology can make a significant contribution, but workers are holding back production. Human resources become the limiting factor even though technology may be more important to overall performance. In these cases it would be best to see how the human factors can be managed so that the employees will adjust to the new technology.

In this stage of the performance audit, the relationship among organizational structure, technology, and human resources should be analyzed to understand the limits each puts on the other. Understanding each separately is not enough. You have to know how they relate to and affect each other. Will changing technology require new human resources? As workers become more specialized and highly educated, will they require different types of technology to be effective? Will different kinds of employees require different structures? How does technology affect structure? If new technology is introduced, will it require a new structure?

You can use the following questions to analyze the relationships among the factors of organizational performance. The purpose of the questions is to determine how the components affect each other and which ones are the most limiting to performance.

1. Where is the idle capacity and slack? Are technology and materials being used to capacity? Are employees devoting all their skills and energy to their jobs?
2. If the technology were upgraded, would there still be unused human potential? Would workers have to be retrained?
3. Could the organizational structure be changed to increase the performance of the present technology? Do the current employees match the needs of the present technology?
4. Are the individuals in the organization grouped in the most productive way possible? Could they be rearranged without changing the technology?
5. Are employees working as effectively as they can? If employee skills and efforts were improved, would performance improve?

Which Component(s) Do You Have Enough Control Over to Improve Performance?

It would seem that once having determined the most important components and understood which ones are limiting performance, the next step is apparent and simple: change the most important component that is limiting performance. Unfortunately, you may not control all the factors of organizational performance. Just because new technology is needed doesn't mean it can be obtained. Just because people don't have the right skills doesn't mean you can train them. Just because the structure isn't working doesn't mean it can be adjusted.

Management is often limited. The technology of your firm may be inadequate, but it is the best available; in that case, you have to do what can be done with the people and the structure and accept the current technology as a constraint. If the people are not quite right for the job, but the labor market is tight, you may not be able to find better employees. You must adjust the structure and technology to make the people as productive as possible. If the structure of your firm isn't functioning well, but you are not high enough in the organization to change it you will have to try to find the people and technology that work best in the current structure.

If the primary constraining factor is an immovable constraint, you have to focus on other factors in the short run. In the short run you accept the things you *cannot* affect, and in the long run you try to change them. The following questions will help you analyze what components of performance you *can* affect.

1. What can be changed on the job without approval from superiors?
2. What can the superiors approve without checking with others? What are they most likely to approve?
3. How long would it take to make effective changes in each of the factors?
4. How long would it be before the changes had an effect on performance?
5. Must subordinates accept a change before it will be effective? If so, how is their acceptance gained?

In summary, the component you should focus your efforts on is determined by the component's importance, how much it is limiting performance, and whether you control it. Human resources should not always be your focus. In fact, if they are constrained by technology and structure, they will have little relationship to organizational performance, and focusing on them will just lead to frustration.

What makes human resources and managing human performance so critical to understand is that people are usually important, they often limit organizational performance, and more significantly, most managers directly control the motivation, effort, and skills of the people who work for them. As a manager you may not be given the decision of what technology you use and the organization structure may be set, but you are the biggest determinant of your employees' motivation. You control much of what allows them to perform, gets them excited about their work, and directs their efforts. That is why the focus of this book is managing human performance, but as we have discovered human performance must be managed within the context of the organization formed by technology, structure, and human resources.

Once you answer the questions in the performance audit, you can design realistic systems for managing within the context of the organization. Figure 3-3 presents a chart for summarizing the analysis. In the chart you rate each of the components on importance, how much they are limiting performance, and the extent to which you control them. The summary provides a guide for decisions on where to focus time and energy. In the short run you should focus on the most *important* component that is *limiting* performance that you *control.* In the long run you try and change some of the constraints.

HOW TO USE THE PERFORMANCE AUDIT

As an example of how to use the performance audit, consider the answers a president of a small electronics firm gave to the questions when asked to audit performance of the assembly department. The organization employs 75 people with 30 in the assembly department, all reporting to one supervisor.

Summary of Performance Audit

Analysis:	Contribution/ Importance	Limitation on Performance	Control
Component Technology			
Structure			
Human resource			

Describe components in each of the categories according to the following scales:

Importance	Limitation	Control
Very important	Very limiting	Very controllable
Moderately important	Moderately limiting	Moderately controllable
Not very important	Not very limiting	Not very controllable
Very unimportant	Not limiting at all	Uncontrollable

Action

Increase performance by improving most important component limiting performance that you control.

Figure 3-3 Summary of the performance audit.

I. What are the relative contributions (importance) of the various factors of performance?

A. Technology

1. HOW MUCH CAPITAL INVESTMENT IS NEEDED TO CREATE AND SUSTAIN THE WORKERS' JOBS?

We make small electronic equipment assembled by hand from components that we purchase from others. We don't use any machinery except the automatic wire clippers and soldering irons in the assembly area. Most of the expense for production is for the materials used and the labor to assemble them. It is not a capital-intensive production operation.

2. HOW DYNAMIC IS THE TECHNOLOGY (I.E., HOW LONG DOES IT TAKE FOR NEW TECHNOLOGY TO BECOME OBSOLETE)?

Our assembly process has not changed during the past seven years. We make state of the art, innovative electronic equipment. New products are always being introduced, but the method of producing them will probably remain the same for quite a while. I don't think we can automate much. We're not that big and are always doing specialized products.

3. TO WHAT EXTENT CAN A COMPETITIVE ADVANTAGE BE GAINED BY USING TECHNICALLY SUPERIOR METHODS?

None. The materials we use already have to meet specifications. Getting higher-quality materials than we need would just add to the expense. We could use some new storage and parts-holding areas, but beyond that I can't think of anything we could do to improve production technologically.

4. IF FINANCIAL CONDITIONS MAKE IT IMPOSSIBLE TO INVEST MONEY IN TECHNOLOGY IN THE FUTURE, WOULD PRODUCTIVITY EVENTUALLY BEGIN TO DECREASE? IF SO, HOW MUCH WOULD IT DECREASE AND HOW FAST?

I don't think productivity would decrease for a long time if all investment in assembly facilities ceased.

B. Structure

1. WHAT PROPORTION (HOW MUCH?) OF THE INPUTS ARE NEEDED FROM OTHER UNITS OR PEOPLE IN ORDER TO ACHIEVE GOOD PERFORMANCE?

   All inputs except the skills of the people of the assembly line come from others in the organization. The engineers determine what the assembly department does and purchasing supplies them with everything we need to make the equipment.

2. HOW MANY OTHER PEOPLE OR UNITS USE THE OUTPUTS OF THE JOB?

   All outputs of assembly go directly to quality control. If they are acceptable, they are shipped to customers. If they are not acceptable, they are returned for repair. Quality control is the only unit the assembly department deals with directly.

3. HOW CRITICAL (HOW IMPORTANT?) ARE THE VARIOUS INPUTS RECEIVED FROM THE OUTSIDE? IS PERFORMANCE DEPENDENT ON THEM?

   The assembly department could not operate without the inputs from purchasing and engineering. They provide all materials and directions on what to do and these inputs are critical to the assembly department.

4. IS PERFORMANCE DEPENDENT ON THOSE WHO ABSORB THE OUTPUTS?

   What the assembly department produces is determined by what quality control will accept. The department has to produce products that meet the quality control standards. If they don't accept them we are in no position to look for alternative users of what the assembly department produces.

5. HOW MUCH DISCRETION DOES THE PERSON DOING THE JOB HAVE IN CONTROLLING:

   a. RESOURCES AND OTHER PERFORMANCE INPUT

   The assembly department has no discretion in determining what we make, what resources they use, or how the product is assembled.

   b. THE MARKET WHERE THE PRODUCT IS DISTRIBUTED

   The assembly department has no discretion in this area: they all go to quality control.

6. HOW MANY RESOURCE SUPPLIERS ARE THERE? HOW MANY OUTLETS ARE THERE FOR THE PRODUCTS OF THE EMPLOYEES' PERFORMANCE?

   There is only one source for their materials and one outlet for their products.

C. Human Resources

1. IS INCREASED EFFORT LIKELY TO LEAD TO INCREASED PRODUCTIVITY?

   Yes, because we assemble everything by hand, employee skills and effort are the main determinants of productivity.

2. HOW MUCH SKILL IS INVOLVED IN THE TASK? DOES IT REALLY MAKE A DIFFERENCE WHETHER YOU HAVE THE RIGHT PEOPLE ON THE JOB?

   Assembling the products takes some coordination skills and dexterity. It is not, however, very complex, most people can learn how to follow the specification provided by engineering in a couple of days. It then takes three to four months to learn the complete procedures and get up to maximum speed. Our experience has been that most people have the skills necessary to perform this job; the biggest determinant of productivity is how hard they work.

II. Which components are presently limiting performance?

1. WHERE IS THERE IDLE CAPACITY AND SLACK? ARE TECHNOLOGY AND MATERIALS BEING USED TO CAPACITY? ARE EMPLOYEES DEVOTING ALL THEIR SKILLS AND ENERGY TO THEIR JOBS?

   There is no idle capacity. The technology is being used to its maximum, and people are working all of the time. The main questions are whether they might be able to increase their efforts and direct them differently.

2. IF TECHNOLOGY WERE UPGRADED, WOULD THERE BE UNUSED HUMAN POTENTIAL? WOULD WORKERS HAVE TO BE RETRAINED?

   I don't think upgrading the technology is feasible. The scale of our operation is not large enough to warrant assembly line procedures with fancy machines. The nature of our products is such that they are always changing and no procedures last for very long. New technology would not make workers more productive.

3. COULD THE ORGANIZATIONAL STRUCTURE BE CHANGED TO INCREASE PERFORMANCE WITH THE PRESENT TECHNOLOGY?

   I think we could make some changes in the structure and improve our performance. Right now, all 30 production workers report directly to the assembly room supervisor. She is always too busy to respond to them. If we had supervisors for every 7–8 people it would work better. I don't mean that we have to hire 3 supervisors, just appoint 3 of the best experienced workers as supervisor of a small group. They could continue to do their own work and be responsible for helping others.

4. ARE THE INDIVIDUALS IN THE ORGANIZATION GROUPED IN THE MOST PRODUCTIVE WAY POSSIBLE? COULD THEY BE REARRANGED WITHOUT CHANGING THE TECHNOLOGY?

   Right now as I said there is one big group of 30 in assembly. If we could rearrange them so that they were working in smaller groups then each group could assemble a complete product. They would have more of a feeling of accomplishment and we could give them better feedback, because we could better locate mistakes.

The technology does not prevent this arrangement. There would have to be some rearrangement in the physical layout of the production floor. It would be organized according to the production group instead of randomly as it is now.

5. ARE EMPLOYEES WORKING AS EFFECTIVELY AS THEY CAN? IF EMPLOYEES SKILLS AND EFFORTS WERE IMPROVED, WOULD PERFORMANCE IMPROVE?

I think so. The quality and quantity of the output is almost completely determined by the skills and motivation of the employees. Any improvement in skills and any effort would have an immediate and direct effect on output.

III. Which factor do you have enough control over in the short and long term that you can change it to improve performance?

1. WHAT CAN BE CHANGED ON THE JOB WITHOUT APPROVAL FROM SUPERIORS?

I can change the organizational structure within production. If I want to put them in three groups, I could. I can work on improving the skills of the people in production. I can hire and fire. I can't make technological changes in the short run. The board of directors would have to approve any major changes.

2. WHAT CAN THE SUPERIORS APPROVE WITHOUT CHECKING WITH OTHERS? WHAT ARE THEY MOST LIKELY TO APPROVE?

The assembly supervisor can approve changes in structure for the department she supervises. She can also approve technological charges up to $1000. I, as president, must approve expenditures beyond $1000. She cannot approve expansion in the number of positions in her department. Only I can approve new positions.

3. HOW LONG WOULD IT TAKE TO MAKE EFFECTIVE CHANGES IN EACH OF THE FACTORS?

Small technological changes can be made as quickly as the materials and equipment can be purchased. If the organization gets big enough or switches to products that require large-scale assembly equipment, there will need to be large capital expenditures. With the present technology, changes can be made quickly.

Structural changes within production can be made immediately. I wouldn't do it any faster than the group could accept but that is the only thing that would slow us down. Changes in structure outside of production, that is, our relationships with other units, would take longer. Tradition has been built up over seven years; any changes in the relationships among departments would probably meet with considerable resistance.

Human resources could also be changed fairly quickly if I wanted to go the hire and fire route. I don't think I would do that, however, We have a good group here already, I think that it is just a matter of getting them organized better and redirecting their efforts.

4. HOW LONG WOULD IT BE BEFORE THE CHANGES HAVE AN EFFECT ON PERFORMANCE?

The length of time it would take for technological changes to have an effect on performance will be determined by how long it takes those in production to learn how to use the new technology.

Changes in human resources will have an effect as soon as the changes are made. If we were to get new people, they would immediately start having an effect. If we were to improve the skills of the people we have, it will take some time for them to learn new skills. Structure changes are likely to take longer to have an effect. People will have to get used to new ways of working with each other.

5. MUST YOUR SUBORDINATES ACCEPT A CHANGE BEFORE IT WILL BE EFFECTIVE? IF SO, HOW CAN YOU GAIN THEIR ACCEPTANCE?

> I don't think any change will work unless it is accepted by those actually doing the work. I guess the best way to gain their acceptance is to involve them in deciding on and implementing the changes.

Figure 3-4 presents the summary for the assembly department in the electronics firm. This performance audit indicates that the manager ought to focus in the short run on the structure of the workforce within the production department, and in the long run, the structure of the whole organization should be revamped. Technology does not seem to be important in the assembly department and in the short run anyway is not changeable. The skill and energy of the employees is important, but the president seems to feel that they are doing well. The way they are organized should be changed. In fact, the firm is a good example of what would happen if the focus were on the wrong factor of performance. More pressure for production, incentive systems, training, or other programs aimed at improving the employees performance without changes in the structure will lead to negative results. Right now they don't identify with a product, receive no feedback, and have no way of correcting their mistakes. Changes in the organizational structure can greatly improve the situation.

SUMMARY

The performance audit determines the relative contributions of each of the components of organizational performance: technology, structure, and human resources. To determine which of these need management attention, ask the following three questions.

Summary of Performance Audit

Analysis:	Contribution/ Importance	Limitation on Performance	Control
Component			
Technology	Not very important	Not limiting at all	Very controllable
Structure	Very important	Moderately limiting	Very controllable
Human resource	Very important	Not very limiting	Moderately controllable

Action

Revise structure within production department to allow full utilization of human resources.

Figure 3-4 Summary of the performance audit for an electronics firm.

1. What are the relative contributions of each component?
2. Which components are limiting performance?
3. Which components do you have enough control over to improve performance?

FOUR
STANDARDS AND MEASURES OF PERFORMANCE

Now that we have discussed the three factors determining organizational performance—human resources, technology, and structure—we are going to focus on one of them: human performance. Throughout the discussion you should remember the importance of the other two factors: technology and structure. In the performance audit, you may have found that organizational performance can best be improved by changing technology and structure. If so, you should become familiar with the techniques for managing these factors. In the rest of this book, we will touch on them as they are important for managing human resources but we will not cover them in depth. To be concise and avoid repetition in the rest of this book, whenever we talk about performance we are referring to human performance.

In order to manage human performance, some way of setting standards and measuring, analyzing, and assessing situations and the people against those standards needs to be established. Because most jobs are too complex to be dealt with in their entirety, setting standards, measuring, and analyzing involve summarizing. Too much is happening for us to take account of everything. We have to decide what is important and focus our attention on that. We have to collect data that accurately defines and summarizes a whole series of activities and results. These summaries will usually involve quantification, categorization, and description of some sort. They may be either quantitative or qualitative. They may include cost and profit information or describe such things as feelings and attitudes. Whatever they are, these summaries serve as the basis on which decisions are made.

Numerous ways exist for measuring, collecting, and interpreting human performance. In this chapter, we identify several ways to do this and then suggest some rationale for choosing among them. In this discussion performance standards should be thought of as definitions of what is to be accomplished. Performance measures are summaries of what is happening toward accomplishing those standards. Performance standards identify targets; performance measures summarize progress toward the targets.

HOW CAN PERFORMANCE BE DEFINED AND MEASURED?

Standards and measures can focus on any or all of the stages of the performance process, ranging from skills and resources to results and feedback. Standards and measures can also vary according to their subjectivity, that is, the influence of the data collector on the data themselves. Consider subjectivity first and then look at specific techniques that can be used to summarize and assess each of the performance stages.

Subjective Versus Objective Data

One way in which standards and measures vary is according to the degree of subjectivity involved. Data that are quantitative and verifiable are considered objective. The overall distinguishing characteristic of objective data is that they are not subject to individual interpretation, that is, they do not vary according to the person doing the measuring. Because objective data are "count data" they can often be collected through mechanical means. Objective data are standardized and homogeneous. Production, which can be counted in units, and financial data, which can be counted in dollars, are two of the best examples of objective data.

Note specifically that objectivity implies nothing about the meaning of the data; that is a separate issue. Even with data such as units produced and dollars earned, there are variations in meaning; for instance, accountants use many different ways of collecting, reporting, and interpreting financial data. The final dollar amount of profit or number of units produced by a firm may be an aggregate of many types of data. Even though the number itself may be objective, it does not vary according to who is doing the collecting, numerous subjective judgments may have been used in deciding what was to be collected, how it was to be aggregated and reported. These judgements need to be understood before the data can be understood.

The advantage of objective data is that they do not vary according to the person collecting them. Different people measuring the same situation will obtain the same results. No perceptual biases exists in the collection of the data. We may not agree on what the data means but at least we will agree on what the data are. Objective data also provide fairly concrete information on the material characteristics of an organization. We can know how many typewriters a unit has, how big the offices are, how much money it has to work with, what the turnover rate is, etc. Data of this kind identify the objectives, resources, and organizational characteristics that can be changed to improve performance.

The disadvantage of objective data is that they don't indicate how the person who is collecting and/or using them is interpreting the situation. Even if the data are objective, the managers and employees still have to evaluate their meaning. They still have to react based on what they think their meaning is, and that reaction will be a subjective one.

Subjective data are perceptual ratings that involve people's interpretations and judgments. Because subjective data are perceptions, they vary according to the rater. A supervisor who is asked to rate the promotion potential of his or her subordinates on a scale from (1) to (7) for instance, generates subjective data. Who the supervisor is and how he or she views the employee will effect the rating in two ways. First, the supervisor's definition of promotion potential will affect the rating. It may even be that what he or she means by that term is very different from what the employee means. The supervisor will fill out the rating based on his or her definition and the employee will interpret this data based on his or her definition. Yet, when they are discussing the rating, both will probably assume that they are defining promotion potential in the same way.

Subjectivity also enters into data through the rating scale. What does a "3" rating on promotion potential mean? Again, the supervisor and the employee may interpret that "3" very differently. Because of these two distortions, what the final rating means is often not clear.

The main advantage of subjective data is that they are indications of how the rater perceives the situation. Like it or not, all of us base our actions on our perceptions of the world. Supervisors and subordinates alike make decisions based on their own interpretations of what goes on in the workplace. By understanding people's perceptions, we can better understand their actions. If we make our impressions and judgments public, then others can challenge us, and we can correct ourselves, or we can at least gain a better understanding of why other people see situations differently.

Because of the different advantages of subjective and objective measures, both should be used. The objective measures provide a sense of what some of the characteristics of the organization are. The subjective measures provide an indication of how the performer is perceiving and responding to these organizational characteristics.

Techniques for Defining Standards and Measuring Progress for Different Stages in the Performance Process

In addition to their degree of subjectivity, another way that standards, measures, and the techniques for collecting them vary is the stage of the performance process on which they focus. The following examples discuss techniques that are used to set standards and obtain data about the different stages of performance. For each stage, the standard is established and progress measured against that standard.

Input or Predictive Standards and Measures Trait, personality, and skills tests are examples of techniques used to assess human inputs into performance. The more traditional way of referring to these inputs is as predictors of performance because workers with poor skills are predicted to do poorly, while workers with excellent skills are predicted to do well. These tests measure characteristics that the employee brings to the job. Input measures run the full range from subjective to objective, but subjective trait ratings have been the most widely used. Figure 4-1 presents an example of a typical subjective trait measure. Standards are set for levels of traits and progress measured in terms of achievement of desired levels.

The field of psychology offers many ways of measuring individual char-

EMPLOYEE PERFORMANCE EVALUATION

Name of Employee	Title and Grade	Organizational Unit
Name of Evaluator	Position Title and Grade	Organizational Unit

Period Covered by This Evaluation
From: ______ Month ______ Day ______ Year To: ______ Month ______ Day ______ Year

EVALUATION	RATER	SECOND-LEVEL SUPERVISOR
1. Job Knowledge	______	______
2. Work Products	______	______
3. Working Relationships	______	______
4. Dependability	______	______
5. Promotion Potential	______	______
6. Judgment and Problem Solving	______	______
7. Adaptability and Creativity	______	______
8. Coordination	______	______
9. Communication Tools	______	______
10. Administrative Ability	______	______
Total	______	______

Adjusted Score ______

EMPLOYEE COMMENTS I have read and discussed the evaluations of the rater and my second-level supervisor. Following are my comments:

Signature ______________________

Figure 4-1 Sample trait measures.

acteristics that are less influenced by the rater than these subjective trait measures. Tests of sensory, perceptual, and other individual characteristics are available. Differences in intelligence and more narrowly defined intellectual processes—such as memory, judgment, and problem solving—have been demonstrated by hundreds of tests.

Both objective and subjective measures of people's skills and traits are appropriate if used correctly. However, management tends to use subjective measures too often because they are quick, cheap, and available, rather than because they are the proper focus. This does not mean subjective measures are not valuable. Sometimes that is the proper focus of management. For example, as a manager, you may wish to increase the satisfaction of your employees. You want to build a sense of cohesion in work groups. As a method you decide to conduct team-building sessions where perceptions, impressions, and feelings, particularly about each other, are discussed and assessed. In this case, you should use subjective measures of involvement, satisfaction, and attitude toward the group. Perceptions, attitudes, and feelings are what you are working on and that is what you should be measuring.

Process and Activity Standards and Measures Activity standards and measures focus on what people do on the job. They are concerned with the way people go about their work and how they interact with others. Ways of collecting process information have taken a variety of forms. One approach has been narratives or essay appraisals (Oberg, 1972). These are written descriptions of what an employee does on the job. The main problem with this approach is it is so individualized that comparisons of different employee's performance is impossible.

Behavioral checklists and critical-incident techniques were developed as a way of standardizing ratings to compare employees' work on the job. The behavioral checklist provides a list of possible behaviors from which the evaluator checks the ones that he or she observes the performer doing. The critical-incident technique asks the evaluator to describe behaviors that he or she observes. Smith and Kendall (1963) combined the advantages of the behavioral checklist and the critical-incident approach and developed the Behaviorally Anchored Rating Scales (BARS). The categories and descriptions included in BARS are developed by those who are actually on the job. Because they participate in the development of scales, they have a better understanding of what is being rated. A list of steps for developing BARS are presented in Figure 4-2.

Remember that the main difference between the process scales and the trait scales is their focus on different stages of performance. For example, interpersonal ability may be considered in both approaches. In the trait approach, the question asked is, "What kind of interpersonal skills does

1. Orientation to BARS purpose and terminology: meetings of about two hours for each group used. Groups of 20 to 30 are most effective.
2. Identification of all relevant job dimensions: meetings of about two hours for each group of 20 to 30 used.
3. Writing behavioral anchors for each job dimension illustrative of various degrees of performance: about one hour for each participant for *each* job dimension.
4. Attach randomized group of anchors back to job dimensions: about two hours for each participant.
5. Deciding on scale values for remaining anchors: about two hours for each participant (can be combined with step 4 above).
6. Computing percentage of participants who agree on placement of anchors to job dimensions and mean scale value given each anchor by participants: time required varies depending on number of anchors and participants. (Electronic calculators simplify the process greatly.)
7. Arranging anchors surviving step 6 above on scales according to appropriate scale value and job dimension: time required depends on number of anchors and job dimensions.
8. Reading over final scales to assure proper terminology, adding any necessary anchors, final editing, etc.: time required varies according to number of job dimensions used and number of people involved in this stage.

Figure 4-2 Steps required to develop BARS and approximate time required. (*Source:* C. E. Schneier and R. W. Beatty, "Developing Behaviorally Anchored Rating Scales (BARS)," *Personnel Administrator,* August 1979, The American Society of Personnel Administration, 30 Park Drive, Berea, OH 44017.)

this person have?" In the behavior approach, the question is "What interpersonal behaviors do I see this person exhibiting?" In the first case, the rating is of an individual characteristic. In the second, the rating is of behavior observed on the job. Figure 4-3 gives an example of a behavior scale used to rate how effectively a department store manager supervises sales personnel.

More objective ways of defining and measuring processes also exist. Bales (1956) developed interaction process analysis as a method of observing how people interact with each other using a sophisticated counting system. Mintzberg's observations of chief executives involves an elaborate procedure for counting time spent on various activities.

Output Standards and Measures Output standards and measures focus on the results of the performance process. Figure 4-4 is an example of a typical output-oriented approach. Traditionally output approaches have used objective physical measures of quantity and quality of production. However, the performance process produces other results, both objective and subjective, that management should be concerned about: for example, a change in the attitude, an increase in skill, or a feeling of satisfaction in the worker. Those who perform poorly may become discouraged and withdrawn and that will affect their ability to perform next time. Output measures should run the full range of results desired by the organization.

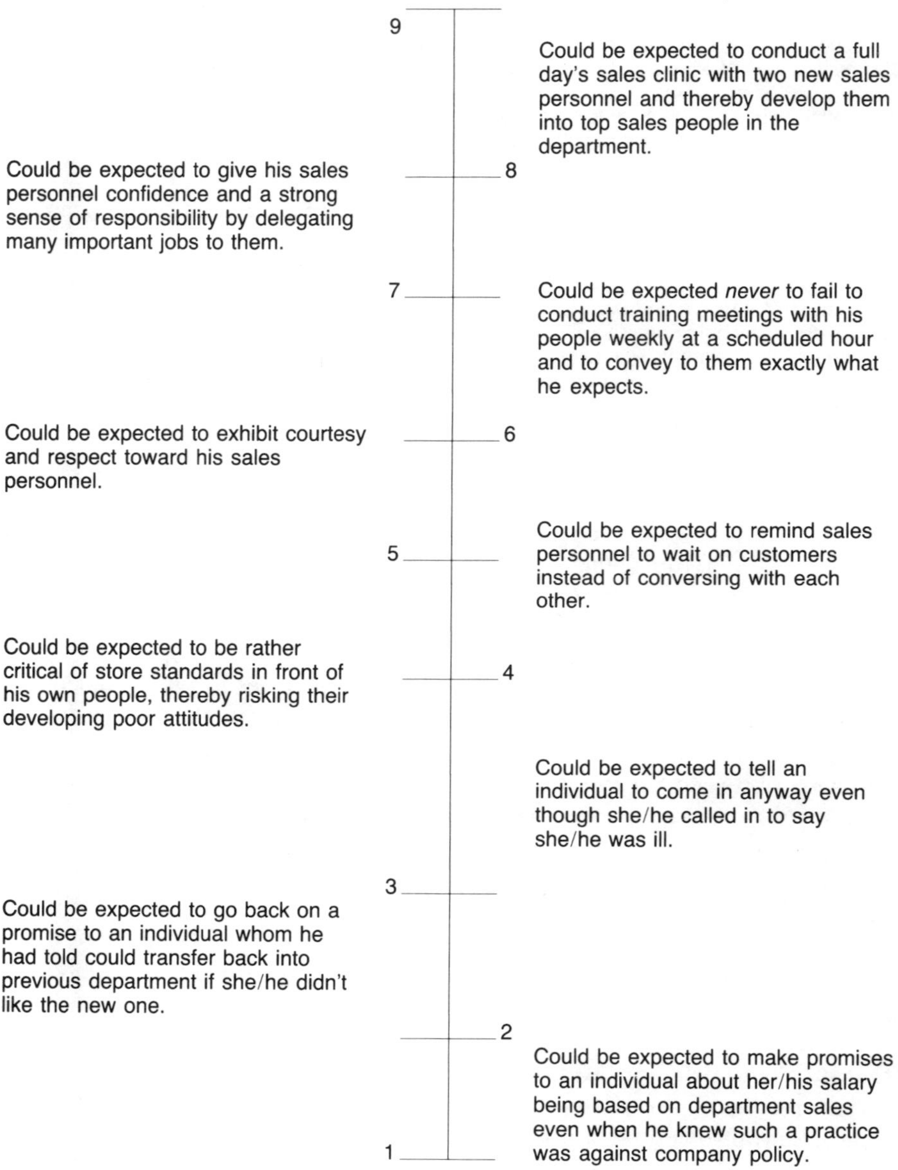

Figure 4-3 Sample behavioral measure. (*Source:* J. P. Campbell, M. D. Dunnette, R. D. Arvey, and L. V. Hellervik, "The Development and Evaluation of Behaviorally Based Rating Scales," *Journal of Applied Psychology,* 1973, *57,* 15–22.)

Sam Speedy		General Manager	Progress Reviews
Prepared by Manager	Date	Position Title	1st ____ 2nd ____ 3rd ____
Harry Slow		Production	
Reviewed by Supervisor	Date	Position Title	

MAJOR JOB OBJECTIVES	% WT	MEASURES OF RESULTS	STD. OF PERF.	RESULTS Target	RESULTS Actual	DATES Target	DATES Actual
1. PRODUCT DELIVERY (May be broken down by products)	25%	a. Percent of on-schedule delivery			94%	Increase to 98%	8/31
		b. Number of customer complaints as a % of monthly purchase orders			4%	Decrease to 3%	9/30
2. PRODUCT QUALITY (May be broken down by products)	30%	a. Percent of rejects per total monthly volume			6%	Decrease to 4%	7/31
		b. Ratio of factory repair time to total production hours/month			7%	Decrease to 4%	9/31
		c. Number of units service free during warranty period			73%	Increase to 86%	10/31
3. OPERATING EFFICIENCY	25%	a. Cost per unit of output per month			$35.75 unit	Reduce to $35.50 unit	2/1
		b. Equipment utilization time as a % of monthly available hours			86%	Increase to 95%	11/5
4. OTHER KEY OBJECTIVES	20%						

Figure 4-4 Sample outcome measure. (*Source:* From R. W. Beatty and C. E. Schneier, *Personnel Administration: An Experiential/Skill-building Approach,* Addison-Wesley, Reading, Mass., 1981, p. 156.)

WHICH STANDARDS AND MEASURES TO CHOOSE?

Figure 4-5 summarizes the discussion up to this point. The focus of management practices—and hence the measurement techniques used to gather data for decision making—can vary by virtue of (1) the stage of performance process on which they focus and the (2) degree of subjectivity or personal interpretation involved in the ratings.

As presently used, the techniques for setting standards and measuring performance have tended to lump together along a diagonal in Figure 4-5. Input standards and measures have traditionally been narrowly defined as traits and have been measured by subjective rating scales. Input standards and measures have rarely included assessments of organizations or groups. Nor have they included assessments of specific skills and traits by more objective measurement techniques.

Activity and process standards and measurement techniques have also tended to be subjective but the use of BARS, critical incidences and the like have made them less subject to individual interpretation. More objective techniques are available, such as those of Bales or Mintzberg, that can be used. Time and motion studies were used in the past as more objective ways of measuring work processes and could be used even though they have recently lost favor because they seemed to dehumanize the employee's work.

Output standards and measures have tended to be the most objective. Led by Management by Objective (MBO) proponents, outcome measures which are not objective, were seen as not useful.

From our discussion, it should be apparent that many different types of standards and measurement are possible. There is nothing inherently good or bad about using any particular type. Nothing about objective or subjective measures or measures focusing on any particular stage of performance makes them necessarily better than other types of measures. Measures are good or bad, depending on what you are trying to manage. The technique

	Inputs	Activities and Processes	Outcomes
Subjective	Trait scales		
		BARS and process-oriented scales	
Objective			Goal-oriented scales

Figure 4-5 Type of standards and measures used in management practices.

for setting standards and measuring progress you should use depends on what you are trying to accomplish, and your focus. If you are responsible for recruiting, the measure of your success is the number and quality of the employees you find. The techniques you use to set standards and measure your performance should focus on those factors. If you are trying to change the way people work with each other, the standards you set and use to measure your progress should focus on how they relate to each other. If you are trying to improve people's satisfaction with their work, the standards and measures should focus on their perceptions and attitudes towards work.

If the situation is not appropriate, subjective input standards and measures (e.g., traits) should not be used just because they are cheap and available. If you are responsible for finishing a certain project to meet specifications and a deadline, you know what to do and the way to get it done is predictable; outcomes of successful project completion are the appropriate measure of your performance. Professional ability as rated by your supervisor is not the appropriate measure of your success. Professional abilities are skills you bring to the job that may or may not be related to the actual results you accomplish. For you to be evaluated solely on your professional ability can only lead to problems.

In summary, there are four points to remember about standards and measurement techniques.

1. As a manager you decide on what part of the performance process to focus. You may decide that inputs, processes, results, or any combination are the appropriate aspects of performance to measure. What you need to do is make sure your standards and measures are consistent with the requirements of performance.
2. Objective and subjective measures have advantages and disadvantages. You have to decide your focus. If you are interested in attitudes, perceptions, feelings, etc. then you will probably want to use subjective standards and measures. If you are interested in physical characteristics, you will probably want to use objective standards and measures. Keep in mind that both objective and subjective measures have their advantages. Objective standards and measures provide a description of the physical characteristics of the organization. Subjective standards and measures show how people are perceiving and responding to occurrences in the work place.
3. No matter on what part of the performance process you focus, the other components of the performance process cannot be totally forgotten. Standards and measures of them will be important in order to diagnose and correct problems.
4. Your standards and measures should be consistent, that is, progress toward an output standard is best determined using output measures.

THE ACCURACY OF YOUR MEASURES

Whenever we summarize, no matter what stage of the performance process, the question arises of how accurately we have represented the situation. We can borrow from statistical methodology to explain what accuracy is, how it can be determined, and why it is important. Most of what we will talk about will refer to objects that can be counted in some way. This is because the concepts of accurate measurement come from statistics. The concepts do, however, also apply to words, colors, codes, or anything else that is used to summarize a situation.

Two terms from statistics that can be used to describe accuracy are validity and reliability. Validity asks the question "Does the data really measure what it is supposed to?" Reliability asks "Will the results be the same if we measure the person, situation, etc. again?" Let us consider each of these characteristics carefully.

Validity

A valid measure is one that is a good summary of a situation. Three questions can be asked to help investigate a measure's validity.

1. What is being measured?
2. What does the measure mean?
3. How are the data collected?

What Is Being Measured? Measures are numbers, words, or statements that summarize a situation. Whenever summaries are used, the question of whether they are truly representative of the whole situation is raised. Before this can be judged, what the "whole situation" is must be understood; in validation studies this concept is referred to as the "performance domain." Using our terminology, the performance domain consists of the job and the goals or desired results.

For a bank officer in charge of savings accounts, increasing passbook savings accounts and the advertising and interest rates that make it possible is the performance domain. A 20 percent increase in passbook savings might be the specified standard. An accounting system that identifies the present number of savings accounts and tracks their growth is the way progress might be measured.

To develop accurate measures of performance, the logical sequence of steps to be followed is (1) define the performance domain (i.e., what is the job and its goals), (2) develop standards of good performance, and (3) establish ways of measuring progress towards the goals.

This sequence is often not followed. Many companies do not do any analysis of the jobs before developing performance appraisal systems. These companies developed measures and collected data without clearly defining what they wanted to measure. In this case, it would be impossible to justify their measures as good summaries.

If the performance domain has been clearly identified, the following questions can be answered affirmatively.

1. Has the job been analyzed and thoroughly described?
2. Is there a clear understanding of the standards of good performance?
3. Is the measure used consistent with the nature of job? (If the desired results are multidimensional, the measures should be multidimensional. If the desired results are subjective, the measures should be subjective.)

What Does the Measure Mean? The validity of measures can also be investigated by looking carefully at what a measure means. When an employee says, "Sales are down", what does he or she mean? Does it mean beginning inventory minus ending inventory is higher this quarter than last quarter? Does it mean accounts receivable plus cash sales are low? Does it mean cash received for this period minus bad debts from last period are less than what was expected? Is the final measure for sales, a weighted summation of sales for different product lines or is it a count of one product line? The phrase, "Sales are down" in and of itself is not useful for performance management. Descriptive and meaningful information must be available.

Determining what a measure means is not as easy as might seem. One must constantly question what is being counted and continually attempt to understand what a high or low score means. Answers to the following questions will help investigate what a measure means.

1. What is being counted?
2. What are the subgroups or measures that are aggregated to obtain the final overall score?

How Are the Data Collected? Measurement systems must have some basic characteristics in order to provide accurate data.

1. The system must record both positive and negative aspects of performance. This might be compared to a thermometer that covers the full range of possible temperatures rather than stopping at zero. In other words, the system must be able to track performance wherever it goes.

2. The measurement must be appropriately calibrated. Knowing how many dollars rounded to the nearest thousand a small hardware store has

invested in stock won't help management know what to order. On the other hand, the exact inventory of a major multinational firm will be too cumbersome to be useful.

3. The measures should be taken as soon as possible after a job has been done. The longer the time period between the performance of a job and the measurement, the more likely it is that the measurement will be distorted. A common example of the effect of time lag on performance measurement is that of the manager who must write a year-end evaluation of a worker without having observed that employee or taken measures of his or her performance throughout the year. The manager may try to remember what has happened during the year, but inevitably events closest to the evaluation will affect it most because that is what the manager can remember best. This will present a very biased picture of the employee's performance. Job performance is best documented during or right after it occurs.

4. Measures should be consistent. They should also be continuously taken and used. Job performance occurs over a period of time and so should performance measurement. Measures used must be able to track changes that occur throughout the time period. They should be taken often enough to provide enough data for an accurate picture of the situation but not so often as to generate more data than can be productively used.

The following questions should be asked about how measurement is being done:

1. Does the measurement cover the full range of possible performance levels from high to low?
2. Are the measures appropriately calibrated?
3. Are the measures taken as soon after the performance as possible?
4. Do the measures track performance over time?

Reliability

A measure is reliable (1) if the same results are obtained when the performance is measured again or (2) if two different ways of measuring the same factor yield similar results. For example, if the suits in a store are counted twice using the same method with the same result, the count is said to be reliable. If the same number of suits is obtained, first by physically counting them and second by adding up the inventory slips, the measures would be considered reliable.

The difference between reliability and validity must be remembered. At the most basic level reliability asks, "If we both measure the same thing twice will we obtain the same results?" Validity asks, "Are we measuring what we purport to be measuring?" Reliability only indicates that results can be duplicated, that you can measure the same thing twice and obtain the same result. This gives you confidence the measure won't vary according to the person doing the measuring or how he or she does it. Reliability is important because it means you can consistently measure something, but reliability won't tell you what is being measured. Just because you can do the same thing twice doesn't mean you are right or that you know what you are doing.

The difference between reliability and validity is important to recognize because the two terms are so often confused. For example, a common defense of subjective performance ratings is that the results obtained by two or more people agree and they must therefore be right. The concept of performance domain can be used to show why this is not necessarily true.

Assume that a loan officer's assignment is to: increase corporate accounts, speed up handling of checks, and improve communication with present accounts. Methods are available for measuring each goal. The number of new corporate accounts is quantifiable and easily determined, as is processing time for checks. An attitude survey plus a count of the number of complaints received from customers can be used to measure communications with present accounts. Each of these measurement techniques will focus on a separate portion of the performance domain of the job. Now assume that rather than use these measures, the branch manager decides to use a subjective trait form rating employees on traits such as initiative, customer relations, promotion potential, etc. The branch manager and her assistant both rate the loan officer. They both come from a conservative background and have a shared idea of what a good loan officer is. One particular loan officer does not conform to that image. He wears the wrong clothes, keeps the wrong hours, and spends a lot of time out of the bank with corporate accounts. It may be that new corporate accounts are growing faster than they ever have, that check processing is more rapid, and that customers are more satisfied with the bank's services; but this employee still is given a low rating because he doesn't fit the rater's stereotype. Just because the measures are reliable doesn't mean they will provide a valid summary of the loan officer's performance. In order to be valid, measures have to deal with activities and results relevant to performance on the job, that is, in the performance domain.

In summary, reliability is important because it indicates that measures won't vary because of the way they are collected. If the computer count of the number of suits in a store is different than the hand count, there would be real questions about the accuracy of the measures. Reliability is important because it increases our confidence that the count is in fact the number on hand. Validity is important because it helps us understand whether the score measures what we really want to know.

The following questions will help assess the reliability of measures.

1. If the same factors were measured twice, would comparable results be obtained?
2. Do different methods of measuring yield comparable results?

DEVELOPING ACCURATE MEASURES

The characteristics of accurate measures suggest some ways of developing them. For example, if measures are summaries of the whole, the whole must be defined before the summary can be developed. If the same results are supposed to be obtained when the measurement is repeated, the method of measuring must be clear and specific.

The usual way of developing measures doesn't provide these characteristics. Guion (1961) offers the best summary of what is usually done.

1. The managers have a hunch that they should have some type of measures on which to base their decisions; they are receiving all sorts of pressure from the personnel office and the legal department to develop accurate measures of performance.
2. They read some vague, ambiguous description of the job that was developed perhaps 10 years before, that focuses on the qualifications of prospective employees, not on the expected accomplishments of the jobholder.
3. From this ambiguous description they decide what they think should be accomplished on the job. In doing this, they focus on what will be of greatest value to the organization.
4. Being well-trained managers, they realize that there are many things the organization is trying to accomplish. They develop a long list of desired accomplishments. Being practical, they also realize that they must make decisions about whom to promote, transfer, or reward financially. They decide to combine the various measures of promotion potential, training needs, job performance, and transferability into a composite score.
5. They then decide that all of the measures aren't equally important, so they weight the various elements in their summation. This will give each measure (job performance, promotion potential, training needs, etc.) a weight according to its importance.
6. They start collecting the data and find that some of it is not available in the organization's data banks. Some of the information is in the personnel department which is always so busy doing wage and salary record keeping that they won't be able to get it up on the computer.
7. As an alternative, the managers decide to use the "best available measure." Because subjective performance ratings have been done and

recorded in the past they decide to use them until something better is available.

Although events often happen in this sequence, there is a preferred method for developing measures. Admittedly, the preferred method is more expensive and time consuming, but it will result in improved decision making (Nagle, 1955; Guion, 1961). The preferred way begins with an accurate description of the job and then proceeds to the development of the measures. The following is a summary of the suggested procedure.

Step 1: Define the Job

First, the job must be defined. The desired results and activities necessary to obtain them must be specified.

Step 2: Analyze the Job

Next the job must be analyzed to determine what resources and skills go into the performance process, what activities and behaviors are appropriate to accomplish the work, and what the desired results are.

Step 3: Develop Standards of Success

The question at this stage is "What constitutes good performance?" This step should not be taken lightly. Standards are set and the type of data to be collected is determined. Once the standards are specified and the data collected, people tend to focus on them to the exclusion of all else. For example, if the measure of success in a car dealership is the number of new cars sold, that will be the focus of the employee's activity, sometimes to the detriment of customer service, used-car sales, employee training, and quality of sales. If the measure of success in a hospital is dollar profit, that will be the focus of employee activity; patient care, employee training, research and development, etc. may be ignored in the rush for profits. If that is not what you want, then you will have to develop different standards of success.

Step 4: Establish a System to Measure Progress Against the Standards

Once you define the standards for success, establish a system for measuring progress against the standard. The data collected must be consistent with the standard of the job.

Step 5: Implement the System

Developing standards of success and ways of measuring progress is the basis of performance management. Ultimately, however, the contribution made by standards and measurement will be determined by how they are implemented. Here are some suggestions of what can be done to apply standards and measurement properly.

1. Communicate the nature of the standards to the employees. Too often performance measurement becomes an "I gotcha" system. Under the "I gotcha" system, the manager waits until the end of the evaluation period to discuss the performance standards with the employee. Even then, they are not really discussed. Instead, the manager says something like "Bill, you didn't do very well, I'm afraid we are going to have to reassign you unless you can improve your performance next quarter." The employee never does find out what was expected. Employees must understand what is expected of them and know how they will be evaluated early in the game. One very good way to help employees understand what is expected is to involve them in defining good performance and developing the standards. Their involvement will have multiple payoffs; first, if they are already on the job, they will likely know more about what good performance is and how it should be measured than anyone else in the organization. Second, employees are the ones who will be directly involved in working towards the objectives. They need to be committed to using the performance standards to guide activities and behavior. The best way to get commitment is to have them participate in developing the standards and measures.
2. Use the standards as the basis for designing the job. Jobs exist to accomplish something. Goals and standards are a way of describing what that something is. Jobs should be designed so that they can accomplish the desired results.
3. Explain areas of discretion in working towards the desired result. Technology and organizational structure establish the boundaries within which the employee works, but within these boundaries remains an area of discretion in which the employee can decide how and what should be done. Both aspects of the job—those the employees control and those they do not—must be clearly understood by the manager and the employee.

THE DYSFUNCTIONS OF SETTING STANDARDS AND MEASURING PERFORMANCE

Following these guidelines will not always lead to success. Several possible dysfunctions of setting standards and measuring performance should be kept in mind to avoid the adverse effects of misusing the data. Standards and measures of performance only provide targets and data. They do not manage or make decisions, people do. Standards and measures of performance are only potentially useful and constructive. If misused or abused, they can have very adverse effects.

The Tyranny of the Single Standard and/or Measure

Rarely does an operation, unit, group or task have only one outcome, one effect on production or is affected by only one other unit. The outcome of the processing of one bank loan affects the loan officer, the bank, the customer, the market (housing, auto, school) for which the loan was drawn. It affects the organization by reflecting on the loan officer, the branch office, and the lending institution as a whole. The processing of the loan is affected by the financial status of the loanee, the policies of the bank, and the government and the local or national economy.

For this reason, single measures of performance can have adverse effects. If management focuses on only one aspect of performance, such as the number of loans targeted, other aspects may suffer. If individual output is the sole measure, competition will result and intrabranch or intragroup relations may be strained. If overall quarterly output is the sole measure, risks may be stretched, so the long-term survival of the bank is affected. If decreasing bad loans is the sole measure, loan officers may become too conservative; alienating and losing long-term customers. For these reasons, several aspects of any operation should be measured so that the results will be balanced and positive.

Hard Data Preempt Soft Data

People naturally focus on components of the performance process that can be measured with hard data—number of products, dollar sales, and rejection rates—rather than soft data—attitudes, perceptions, and impressions. Hard data always preempt soft data, not because they are better or more important, but because they are easier to add, compare, measure, understand, and tangibly manipulate. Hard data are easier to communicate. Everyone knows what $10, four television sets and 40 tons means.

Soft data are harder to work with. Attitudes, perceptions, and impressions are difficult to quantify and express in equivalent terms. They sometimes require lengthy definitions and subjective explanations. They provoke questions and provide ambiguous answers. Soft data have to be converted to hard before they can be added, aggregated, compared, and communicated. Retaining the spirit and intent of the soft data when converting it to hard is extremely difficult but very important. Accurate understandings of attitudes, perceptions, and impressions are critical to understanding and managing the performance process even though they are soft data.

Everything Is Subjective

New programs or systems put into operation on the basis of collected and analyzed data often have problems or fail because of a common misconception. Many people assume that objective data are more valuable, accurate, and implementable because they do not vary according to the collector. Each person studying a situation will come up with the same results. Subjective data are often considered less valuable or accurate because they do vary according to the collector. Each individual observing the situation will describe and analyze it differently.

These assumptions are partially correct. Subjective data are more varied, more subject to personal interpretation and very difficult to accurately quantify and analyze. On the other hand, what appear to be objective data are not entirely objective. Subjective decisions must always be made in terms of what is to be counted or measured, how this will be done, and how the results will be used. Personal interpretation can cause a crucial set of facts to be omitted or an unnecessary, misleading set to be included. The results can be more damaging than the accurate use of difficult-to-quantify subjective data.

An important point to keep in mind when planning to use data as a basis for decisions is that everything is subjective. Objective data shouldn't be blindly accepted as more accurate, and subjective data shouldn't be categorically condemned. The user of the information should have a clear understanding of how the data were collected, what measures were used, what aspects of the situation were included, and which were omitted. Overly subjective manipulation of objective data is equally as dangerous as overly objective analyzation of subjective data. Only with an accurate understanding of the nature of data can successful and useful decisions be reached.

Short-Term Drives Out Long-Term Performance Standards and Measures

Measures of current and short-term performance will receive more attention than measures of long-term performance. Short-term performance measures are measures of activities and events that happen daily, weekly, and quarterly. They receive more attention than long-term measures, which focus on activities and events that happen yearly, because they seem more controllable and they happen more often. Daily, weekly, and quarterly information is received sooner and much more often than yearly information. Employees will naturally use this short-term information to guide their behavior rather than waiting for the yearly summaries.

Measures of performance must be chosen very carefully to balance short- and long-term needs. Short-term measures should indicate the employee's ability to perform in the long run as well as accomplish the short-term objectives. If the measures do not do this, employees will focus solely on the short run, often to the detriment of the long run. For example, if the objective is to ship 1000 cars and the measures of performance focus solely on the number of cars shipped weekly and quarterly, the shipping department will focus on shipping 1000 cars this quarter. In the process, they may totally deplete their resources, overwork their employees so morale and energy are low, and destroy customer relations, all of which will make it impossible to ship 1000 cars next quarter. The long run is sacrificed to meet the short-run performance objectives. If performance measures included resource levels, morale surveys, and customer relations, employees are much more likely to focus on both short- and long-term results.

Numbers Do Not Make Decisions

Numbers do not make decisions, people do. Data are only information that can be used to make decisions. Unfortunately, once decisions are made and standards set, the numbers take on a life of their own. Regardless of the validity of the original decision, operation results exceeding the set standard are considered successful. Results below standard are considered a failure. Without questioning the standard, just because it has been quantified, the standard is accepted as good.

Serious problems can arise. An accurate interpretation of the original data may have resulted in a standard that was set too high or too low. The nature of the problem may have been misinterpreted, and therefore energy may be misfocused or misdirected. Unfortunately, numerical goals provide concrete direction—something definitive to work towards—whether they are accurate or not. Numerical goals create a feeling that everything is on track.

Numbers are only tools for decision making, they should not dictate behaviors. Measures and data should be checked from several different perspectives, and set standards should be reevaluated regularly. Determining the value and accuracy is always the responsibility of the manager.

SUMMARY

After the appropriate focus of performance standards is decided, the standards must be developed and techniques established to collect data evaluating performance and monitoring progress over time. The techniques of setting standards and measuring progress may vary, but the key to effective management remains defining as specifically as possible what performance is and then selecting measures and collection techniques that summarize it accurately.

Accurate performance measurement is critical to good management. Managers make decisions based on their understanding of occurrences in the workplace and their understanding will be determined by the data collected. We use data in the broadest possible sense, to mean any information, feeling, sense, or attitude that summarizes what is happening. If that summary is not an accurate reflection of reality, the decisions based on it will be wrong.

The accuracy of any standard setting and measurement system is determined by the validity and reliability of the data it generates. To determine how valid and reliable the data are, we must ask what they measure, what they mean, and how they have been collected. To develop accurate performance measures, follow these steps.

1. Define the job and its goals.
2. Analyze the job to determine the resources and skills necessary, as well as the activities and expected results.
3. Develop standards of success that define what constitutes good performance.
4. Establish a system to measure progress against the standard.
5. Implement the system.

FIVE UNDERSTANDING HUMAN PERFORMANCE

INTRODUCTION

In many situations, a critical factor of organizational performance is human resources. People's attitudes and behaviors have a substantial effect on what the organization can accomplish. A motivated workforce often compensates for obsolete technology and inefficient organization. In the rest of this book, we discuss how to manage human performance within the context established by the technology and structure. We begin by showing how people are managed at each stage of the performance process. Then, in subsequent chapters, we consider how systems and procedures can be designed to maximize human performance.

The theories are presented in the sequence of the performance process and provide the rationale for our suggestions of what management should do at each stage: define what is to be accomplished, communicate performance expectations, specify activities, and control rewards and information. Let us review the theories and list questions the theories suggest can be used to understand how each of the components of performance are being managed. These become the background for our recommendations in the rest of the book. Figure 5-1 shows motivation theories that are identified with the appropriate stages of the performance process.

DEFINING AND COMMUNICATING PERFORMANCE EXPECTATIONS

Goal theory (Locke, 1968) has consistently shown the importance of defining and communicating what is to be accomplished. According to this theory, performance is increased two ways when goals are set. First, setting goals directs energy towards them. Instead of wasting physical and psycho-

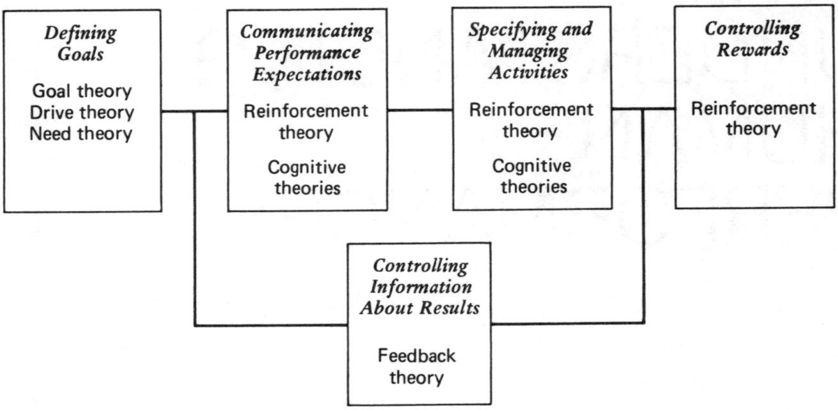

Figure 5-1 Theoretical background for managing human performance.

logical energy on outcomes that will not be rewarding, individuals can focus their actions on important results. Second, the act of setting objectives and directing efforts is energizing. Employees become more involved when they know what they are trying to accomplish.

Considerable research has been carried out testing the relationship between goal setting and behavior. Locke and his associates have conducted many experiments demonstrating that the higher the goal, the higher the performance itself. Locke (1968) also suggests that feedback on results is important because it enables a person to set new goals. Feedback must be given in such a way that goals are not lowered in the face of failure, but maintained and new energy devoted to doing better. Goal theory thus suggests not only the importance of becoming actively involved in the setting of proper goals but also suggests the importance of the manager's understanding the nature and use of feedback.

Employees will be committed to organizational goals to the extent they are consistent with personal goals. Managers thus must understand not only organizational goals but what employees want out of work. Many theories deal with the types of goals employees think are important. The best known of these are drive theory, need theory, and equity theory.

Drive Theory

C. L. Hull (1943) was perhaps the first to use the concept of drives. He defined drives as factors that induce people to behave in certain ways. Hull proposed that behavior was motivated by either primary or secondary drives. Goals are important if they match the drives that people have. Primary drives are related to biological needs. Hull defined objects or events towards which these drives are directed as rewards. The strength of any given drive could be increased by deprivation of that object of desire and then reduced when the object is attained. Hull also recognized a group of secondary drives for which a different set of rewards existed. He believed secondary drives were learned through their association with primary drives; for example, people have a drive to obtain money because they are able to buy food and shelter with it.

Need Theory

Hull's theory proved useful but too restrictive; it could not account for a wide variety of "secondary" drives that did not seem to be related to primary drives. Taking a little different approach, Murray (1938) referred to motivating factors as "needs" and developed a list that included many that Hull's theory had not dealt with. Maslow (1943) did the same and in addition arranged the needs in a hierarchy. Goals are important for the employee if they match the needs they have.

Maslow classified human needs into five levels:

1. Physiological needs—need for water, air, and other things to sustain biological life.
2. Safety—need for security and stability.
3. Love—need for affection and positive social interactions.
4. Esteem—need for a personal feeling of achievement as well as recognition and respect from others.
5. Self-actualization—need for self-fulfillment or the realization of one's potential.

This list is similar to Alderfer's (1969) shorter list of existence, relatedness, and growth (ERG) needs. Maslow also proposed a process by which each of the levels in turn became more important. He said that before the higher level needs become important, the lower level (i.e., physiological and safety needs) must be satisfied. As a need is satisfied, it becomes less important to the individual and the next higher level need becomes more important. Very little research has been able to support this extended hierarchy concept (Lawler and Suttle, 1972). Alderfer (1969), however, offers research to support a two-step hierarchy using the ERG theory. In these two steps, the existence needs must be satisfied first, then the relatedness and growth needs become important; in ERG there is no set order in which the higher-level needs become important. In fact, people are simultaneously motivated by several needs. Alderfer also found that growth or self-actualization needs were not diminished when satisfied; they seemed to remain important. Their influence was diminished only when lower-level existence needs were not satisfied and thus became dominant.

The contribution of need theory to performance management has not been its concept of a hierarchy but its grouping of needs into the categories. This has proven particularly meaningful because the categories of need theory relate well to reward systems and other organizational practices. In organizations, physical and security needs are met by the compensation and benefits provided, social relatedness needs are fulfilled in the interpersonal and group activities that take place, and growth and accomplishment are achieved by responsibility and success on the job.

Of all these needs, the need for success has received perhaps the most attention because it is so directly related to what people do on the job. The fullest investigation of this need has been done through the study of achievement motivation. Achievement motivation has been defined by McClelland (1961) as a need to perform well in relation to standards of excellence. Achievement theory hypothesizes that people are motivated by a desire to achieve and be successful. Research has demonstrated that this is most likely to happen when the task is moderately challenging, when performance depends on skills the individual values, and when there is feedback available.

White (1959) also discusses the desire to succeed by hypothesizing a competence motive. He hypothesizes competence as the individual's capacity to interact effectively with environment and argues that individuals have a need for competence that is separate from the primary needs. His research suggests that organisms will try to cope with their environment for no reason except to gain mastery over it. People can be motivated to perform well by being given challenging, and interesting jobs. Once a job is mastered, the desire for competence is satisfied.

A large body of research has found that individuals need to succeed in order to maintain their own self-image. Research on self-esteem (Korman, 1974), locus to control (Rotter, 1966) and attribution theory (Staw, 1977) have been particularly useful in helping us understand people's desire to succeed and maintain a positive self-image. In general, this research suggests that individuals maintain a positive self-image in several ways. One way is to blame others for poor results (Luginbuhl, Crowe, and Kallan, 1975). Another is to devalue the importance of the activity (Lewis, 1976). The more people value doing well, the more defensive they will become about their failures. Overall, the research suggests that people in general have a desire to succeed and be thought well of. This becomes particularly important as we begin to deal with behavior in organizations.

Equity Theory

Another theoretical approach relevant for explaining personal goals deals with people's desire to be treated fairly. Equity theory states that people want to receive rewards equal to others who are making an equal contribution to the organization. Equity is felt to exist when the ratio of a person's job inputs to organizational rewards is equal to that of other employees.

$$\frac{\text{own rewards}}{\text{own inputs}} = \frac{\text{rewards of others}}{\text{inputs of others}}$$

People want equity and if they think the equation is imbalanced, they will reduce the inequity by altering one or more of the factors. Assume, for example, some employees feel others who aren't doing as much work are receiving relatively more money. In order to get even, they might argue for more pay, quit working so hard, attempt to get others to start working harder, or decide the others really aren't the right comparison group (Adams, 1963; Goodman and Friedman, 1969).

Implication of Theory for Defining and Communicating Performance Expectations

This is not an exhaustive list of theories describing what people want out of work, but it provides a sense of the personal goals employees want to reach. Their goals will be determined by their needs, drives, and desires for equity. Management's challenge for managing performance is to make organizational goals and employees' personal goals consistent.

Based on these theories, the following questions can be used to analyze how setting and communicating performance goals is being managed.

1. Have the goals and performance expectations been established?

List in order of importance the three most important results that should be achieved.
a. ____________________
b. ____________________
c. ____________________

2. Do the performance expectations match the personal goals of the individual employees?

3. Have the performance expectations been clearly communicated?

4. Can people easily find out what they are expected to do?

Describe and rate the ways in which goals or performance expectations are communicated.

	How Effective Do You Think These Methods Are?						
Method	Very Ineffective						Very Effective
1.	1	2	3	4	5	6	7
2.	1	2	3	4	5	6	7
3.	1	2	3	4	5	6	7

SPECIFYING AND MANAGING ACTIVITIES

Two types of theories that can be used to suggest how to manage employees' activities are reinforcement and cognitive theories. Reinforcement theories suggest that behavior is determined by its external consequences.

The individual chooses activities that have been rewarding in the past. Cognitive theorists, on the other hand, suggest that behavior is the result of internal attitudes and cognitions. Individuals choose activities they think they have the skills to do and will result in meeting their personal goals.

Behavioral Explanations of Activities

Reinforcement theories suggest that behaviors (activities) are determined by the environment. In this theory, the consequences of an action determine the probability of that action being repeated. In reinforcement theory, the behavior that an individual chooses is a function of two factors: (1) the stimulus to action presented by the work environment and (2) the consequences of that action. According to reinforcement theory, behavior follows this sequence:

1. A stimulus, which can take many forms, is presented; it may be a request from a supervisor, something inherent in the work itself, an assignment to a task force, etc.
2. Based on the stimulus, the individual enters into activity.
3. The activities produce some type of results.
4. The individual is rewarded by the organization according to the results.
5. The individual enjoys the reward, and this increases the probability that the next time the stimulus is presented, the behavior will be repeated.

B. F. Skinner refers to the responses on which the reinforcer is contingent as an operant. Thus, this explanation of behavior is often referred to as operant conditioning. Operant conditioning assumes that individuals want reinforcers (rewards), explore their environment to locate them, and then engage in those behaviors that will be likely to obtain the rewards. This sequence is as follows.

Stimulus → Activity → Reward

This model includes three important concepts that explain the activities of individuals.

1. First is the sequence of events. Activities are based on the stimuli presented and in turn produce results. People are then rewarded based on the results. Rewards follow results.
2. Second is the definition of reward. Reinforcement theory is concerned with rewards that the individual defines as important. Notice again the individual/organizational split. What the organization obtains from the performance process may not be what the individual wants. The goal

of the organization is to sell its good or services, but the goal of the salesperson may be to achieve the highest possible salary, have a secure job, or work with interesting clients. The individual is the one who determines what is rewarding and not the manager or the organization. When experimental psychologists work with hungry animals, they have the advantage of knowing that food will always be rewarding. What individuals in organizations find rewarding is not always clear. Managers do not always know what rewards will reinforce desirable (from the point of view of the organization) behavior in employees.

3. A third important and little discussed point in reinforcement theory is the assumption that what happens as a result of activities in the present is likely to affect behavior in the future. The same stimulus is more likely to elicit a response in the future because it has resulted in the individual's receiving rewards that he or she valued in the present. Assume a manager (1) asks an employee to participate in a special task force and the employee reluctantly agrees. (2) The employee enjoys the experience because of the rewards he or she receives (recognition, feeling of accomplishment, incentive pay, personal growth, etc.). (3) The manager again asks the employee to participate in a special task force. The employee will probably not be as reluctant to participate the second time.

Reinforcement theories have been used to design successful positive reinforcement programs in both the public and private sector (Hamner and Harnett, 1974). The main focus of these programs has been to affect what people do by controlling the rewards of praise, recognition, and money. According to reinforcement theories, activities are affected by the following.

1. Specifying the desired results.
2. Presenting a stimulus, a request, a promised reward, or an assignment to elicit the desired activity.
3. Rewarding according to the results.

Cognitive Explanations of Activities

A major portion of the theories used in organizational research and practice focus on the cognitive processes of the individual. Cognitive theories deal with attitudes, values, emotions, etc. and assume the internal state of individuals causes them to prefer certain activities to others. The most popular of the cognitive explanations of activities has been expectancy theory.

Toleman (1932) was perhaps the first to offer an alternative to the behaviorists' explanation of behavior. He suggested motivation was caused by the individual's goals and values. Vroom (1964) developed these concepts into an expectancy theory of behavior. In expectancy theory, activities are entered into when people expect that the activities will produce desired results. The theory does not attempt to explain what determines the attractiveness of these results but assumes instead that individuals somehow decide what rewards will be satisfactory to them. People engage in the behaviors they think will obtain these rewards.

Various expectancy models have been proposed (Galbraith and Cummings, 1967; Porter and Lawler, 1968; and Lawler 1973). Although some differences exist among the models, they are all built on common assumptions. In these models, a person's decision to enter into a particular activity is a function of what he/she expects to get out of it. These expectations are based on two factors. First is the belief that if a person enters into the activity, he or she will be able to perform well. This belief is based on the person's perceptions of the situation and past experiences. If past attempts have not been successful, the person will most likely not try again. Expectations are based not only on past performance but on some personality factors as well. Individuals develop a self-image as they grow and develop. This self-image can either be one of competence and ability to deal effectively with the environment or one of failure. Beliefs about oneself constitute one's self-esteem and are an important determinant of performance expectations.

The second determinant of people's willingness to devote effort to a task is their perception of whether the outcome will be rewarding. Again, past experience is the biggest determinant of this perception. If the organization distributes rewards randomly, employees will not expect good performance to be adequately rewarded. Like expectations about performance, expectations about rewards are also influenced by people's individual characteristics. Rotter (1966) has developed what he refers to as the locus of controls scale, which measures people's belief about internal versus external control of rewards. People who believe they can influence what happens to them are likely to see a strong relationship between what they do and the rewards they receive. People who believe they do not control what happens to them tend to think that either other people, luck or fate control their rewards. They will not perceive rewards to be related to performance.

The recommendations from expectancy theory are naturally focused on creating realistic expectations. In organizations, training and modeling can be used to show employees how good performance will be rewarded. Managers can motivate their employees by convincing them first they have the ability to perform and second management does in fact control rewards and will distribute them to those who perform well. The manager does this by (1) finding out what rewards workers value, (2) structuring the job and providing training so the individual can perform well, and (3) providing rewards based on performance.

The assumptions a manager must make to motivate action according to expectancy theory are surprisingly similar to those that would be recommended by reinforcement theory. Both theories state that the relationship between what the organization wants and what the individual wants must be clearly specified. The difference between the two schools of thought is that expectancy theory assumes behavior originates in the thoughts and attitudes of the individual while reinforcement theory assumes it originates in the environment.

Implications of Behavioral and Cognitive Theories for Specifying and Managing Activities

The value of both theories is that they help explain why people do what they do. Notice particularly that neither the cognitive nor the behavioral approaches offer explanations of what individuals value, that is, what they want. That is the focus of goal, drive, and need theories previously reviewed. Cognitive and behavioral theories suggestions for affecting the activities of people are surprisingly similar.

1. Specify and communicate clearly the activities and procedures for accomplishing the objectives.
2. Match the skills people have to the job.
3. Clearly specify the rewards for accomplishing the objective.

Based on cognitive and behavioral theory, we can suggest that answering the following questions will help you analyze if activities are being managed.

1. Have the job procedures been clearly established and explained?
2. Have the skills and abilities people need for the job been specified?
   a. How does the organization find out what skills and abilities people need to do its job?
   b. How are people's skills and abilities matched to the job?
   c. How do people learn new skills they will need on the job?

CONTROLLING REWARDS

As reinforcement theory suggests, what people do is strongly influenced by the consequences of their past actions. One way to affect performance is to affect the consequences. As Rummler (1972) suggests, "Results may be positive, negative, or for all practical purposes, nonexistent. They may also be immediate or long-term, and real or potential. Results come simultaneously from a number of sources including the work itself, subordinates, peers, bosses, and the organizational establishment."

To maintain and improve performance, we must manage its consequences properly. When the consequences of performance are not properly managed, a phenomenon occurs that Kerr (1978) refers to as "Rewarding A while hoping for B." The following examples show what can happen when performance results are not properly managed.

Example 1 The negative consequences of having more than 4 percent scrap on the production line drives many a sane and rational foreman to report only 4 percent when he has 7 percent—and to do extreme things to "bury" that remaining 3 percent scrap. The results to the company will be excessive metal costs, inventory shortage, scheduling headaches, and overtime to meet the inventory storage (Rummeler, 1972).

Example 2 In a state agency, the way to make a little extra money was to work overtime, which was compensated at 1½ times regular pay. Top-level management assigned overtime and extra staff to those departments that seemed to need it to get their work done, thus encouraging employees to stretch out their work as long as possible so they could get the overtime. Even if the employees did not want to work the more than 40 hours necessary to qualify for overtime, they could simply take as much sick leave, annual leave, and personal leave as possible, and make up the lost work at overtime rates. Because the work in these departments was still not getting done, top management assigned them even more overtime, while more productive offices had their budgets and staff cut. Not surprisingly, inefficiency and low productivity were rampant; that is what was being rewarded.

Example 3 The marketing division of a bank decided that the tellers needed a training program designed to help them sell additional bank services, with particular emphasis on personal loans. The training was launched and was a total failure. There were too many negative consequences attendant on "selling" other banking services. For the tellers, the sale of these services increased the number and type of transactions they handled and consequently the chance of errors. It also increased the length of the lines at each window because the tellers were spending more time with each person. Long lines meant impatient customers and concerned management. Branch management was under pressure from top management to build a sizable portfolio of loans. Portfolios could be built faster by making a single $1 million loan to a small corporation than by making many $1000 to $3000 personal loans. There were nothing but negative consequences for tellers to do what they had been trained to do. Consequently they didn't do it (Rummler, 1972).

The preceding examples highlight the importance of analyzing the consequences of performance. Rummler (1972) suggests some general guidelines on how this should be done.

1. People don't just not do something, they are busy doing something else. They do something that is rewarding because what they are supposed to do isn't rewarding. Therefore, it is important to look at the consequences both of what people do that they find rewarding and what they are supposed to be doing that is obviously unrewarding. If behavior is to be changed, positive consequences have to shift so that they are attached to desired behaviors.
2. Specific consequences have more affect on behavior than general ambiguous consequences, because ambiguous consequences are difficult to link to specific behaviors. General company statements like "you may get promoted if you do this extra paperwork," are not as important to the behavior of the individual, as a statement like "you will miss lunch with the group, or the presentation this afternoon won't be prepared if you do not finish that report."
3. Immediate consequences need to be understood separate from long-term consequences. Immediate consequences tend to be more important to behaviors because they are more clearly related to them. There is no time to confuse the relationships. If long-term consequences are important, they need to be actively managed to make their relationship with behaviors clear.
4. The certainty of consequences is an important consideration. The natural tendency is to engage in behavior with a high probability of immediate results and low probability of negative consequences.
5. It is crucial to remember that the person on the job decides whether a consequence is positive or negative. What is important to some people will not be valued by others. For example, some people will be very pleased by the opportunity to present their work to a group, while for others, having to present their work to others would be a negative experience.

Implications of Reinforcement Theory for Controlling Rewards

Reward systems in organizations are complex and varied. No matter how they work, their purpose is the same, to reward and encourage good performance. Reward systems should be critically analyzed according to how well they accomplish that purpose. To control rewards, managers should provide workers something they value as a result of their efforts and accomplishments and managers should make the relationship between what the worker does and accomplishes and the rewards they receive as clear as possible. If performance is low, managers should help the employees develop so they can perform. The following questions will help you determine if rewards are being managed properly:

1. Are there rewards and recognition for good performance?
2. Is there assistance and encouragement for poor performance?
3. Describe what happens to good performers.
4. Describe what happens to bad performers.
5. Will what happens to good and bad performers maintain and increase their motivation and performance in the future?

CONTROLLING INFORMATION ABOUT RESULTS

How do people find out how they are doing? Unfortunately the answer to that question is all too often, they don't find out at all. When management adopts a "no news is good news" strategy, the only time employees receive feedback is when their performance is terrible. Then the manager really lets the employee know it. In order to be effective, performance feedback has to be constantly available to the employee. Feedback and evaluation are not activities that can happen once a year. They have to be part of the continuing process of management. Without evaluation and feedback, employees are left to their own devices to figure out how they are doing. Sometimes what they come up with will be accurate, at other times it will be quite different than the evaluation that someone else might give.

Often performance can be dramatically improved by providing the proper feedback. The following is a good example of what can be done by simply letting workers know how they are doing. A vice president of a shipping company was concerned about the productivity of the dock workers. Containers were to be as filled as possible with packages going to the same destination. Shipping containers would cut handling costs and result in an $20 average savings over the costs of shipping the packages individually. At one location, only 10 out of a possible 30 containers were being used each day—a $104,000 annual loss in savings.

After observing the workers, the vice president found that they were familiar with how to use the containers but had no clear performance standards and no feedback. To rectify this situation, a standard of 95 percent container usage was established and communicated to the workers, and a chart was posted on which the number of containers used each day was compared to the number available. The workers were taught how to monitor their own performance. In one week after the feedback system was implemented, performance climbed from 30 percent to 86 percent of the established standard. The employees could just as easily do the job right as do it wrong once they found out what was expected and on how they were doing (Rummler, 1972).

Vroom (1964) identifies three functions that feedback serves: directive, tutorial, and rewarding. Directive feedback matches closely the first phases of performance. Its purpose is to keep the organization and employee on course, that is, to maintain behavior that is directed at the proper goal. The tutorial function of feedback focuses on improving skills and behaviors. This fits the activity stage of performance. Rewarding feedback reinforces employees' good performance.

Research has found that each of these functions is useful in different situations. For example, in tasks where learning is to take place, information that focuses on skills and behaviors is the most useful. In situations where employees know what to do and how to do it, the rewarding function of feedback becomes the most important.

Additional research suggests that a person's response to feedback will also be determined by how it is given. Greller and Herold (1975) for example studied comparison versus task–goal feedback. Comparison feedback compared an individual's performance to others doing the same work. Task–goal feedback, on the other hand, was given relative to some absolute standard. The results were predictable. When comparison was given, employees were likely to engage in competitive behaviors. When task–goal feedback was provided, employees were more concerned about accomplishing the goal.

Comparable results have also been found in experimental research. McClintock and McNeil (1966) found that subjects played significantly more competitively when they were able to compare their own scores with those of others. Drawing from their work and from that of others (McClintock, 1972; Messick and McClintock, 1968), they identified four types of feedback, each of which results in different types of behavior. (1) Individual feedback results in behavior oriented toward maximizing one's own gain. (2) Competitive feedback (comparison of the performance of two people) results in attempts to maximize one's own gain relative to that of others. (3) Cooperative feedback (evaluation of the work of two or more people combined) results in attempts to maximize joint productivity. (4) Altruistic feedback (information about the performance of another person) results in attempts to improve the other person's performance. Clearly managers should give the type of feedback that encourages behaviors most likely to result in job performance.

Implications of Feedback Theory

To manage performance, managers should not only provide feedback about activities and results but they should provide ways for the employees to monitor and evaluate themselves. The following will help you analyze how feedback is being managed.

1. List and rate according to effectiveness the three most important ways people on the job find out how they are doing.

Method	How Effective Are These Methods for Letting Employees Know How Well They Are Doing? Very Ineffective						Very Effective
1.	1	2	3	4	5	6	7
2.	1	2	3	4	5	6	7
3.	1	2	3	4	5	6	7

2. Describe briefly how employees monitor and evaluate themselves.

SUMMARY

Human resources are a critical component of performance. What makes human resources particularly important is that they can be directly affected by what management does. Human resources are often the most controllable of all of the factors of performance and directly relate to what is accomplished. Figure 5-2 summarizes the recommendations theory makes for managing performance.

The questions developed in the chapter are included in Figure 5-3 and can be used to understand human performance and how it is being managed on the job, using the theories in this chapter as background. We will look at each of the components in the rest of the book.

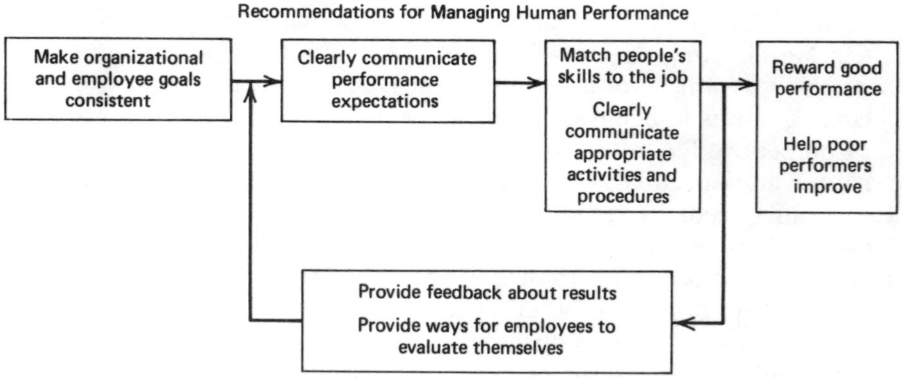

Figure 5-2 Recommendations for managing human performance.

Understanding Human Behavior

I. Establishing and Communicating Performance Expectations

1. Have the goals, performance expectations, been established?

List in order of importance the three most important results that should be achieved.

a. ______________________________

b. ______________________________

c. ______________________________

2. Do the performance expectations match the personal goals of the individual employees?

3. Have the performance expectations been clearly communicated?

4. Can people easily find out what they are expected to do?

Figure 5-3 Understanding human behavior.

Describe and rate the ways in which goals or performance expectations are communicated.

Method	How Effective Do You Think These Methods Are? Very Ineffective						Very Effective
1.	1	2	3	4	5	6	7
2.	1	2	3	4	5	6	7
3.	1	2	3	4	5	6	7

II. Directing Activities

1. Have the job procedures been clearly explained?

2. Have the skills and abilities people need for the job been specified?
   a. Explain briefly how the organization finds out what skills and abilities people need to do its job.

   b. How are people's skills and abilities matched to the job?

Figure 5-3 (*Continued*)

c. How do people learn new skills they will need on the job?

III. Controlling Rewards

1. Are there rewards and recognition for good performance?

2. Is there assistance and encouragement for poor performance?

3. Describe what happens to good performers.

Figure 5-3 (*Continued*)

4. Describe what happens to bad performers.

5. Will what happens to good and bad performers maintain and increase their motivation and performance in the future?

IV. Controlling Feedback

1. List and note according to effectiveness the three most important ways people on the job find out how they are doing.

Method	How Effective Are These Methods for Letting Those on the Job Know How Well They Are Doing? Very Ineffective						Very Effective
1.	1	2	3	4	5	6	7
2.	1	2	3	4	5	6	7
3.	1	2	3	4	5	6	7

2. Describe briefly how employees monitor and evaluate themselves.

Figure 5-3 *(Continued)*

SIX
ESTABLISHING AND COMMUNICATING PERFORMANCE EXPECTATIONS

INTRODUCTION

We receive information about what to do and accomplish in a job from many sources. Superiors, peers, acquaintances, and the environment in general all make demands on us. Sometimes these demands are complementary, at other times conflicting. The supervisor expects high-quality production, peers a manageable work pace, acquaintances at work help with their personal problems, and inspectors from government agencies compliance with safety standards. Somehow we have to balance all these expectations.

DESIRED RESULTS: WHAT IS THE WORKER EXPECTED TO ACCOMPLISH?

Desired results or performance expectations are limited only by the imagination of the people involved and the environment in which they work. They can range from tangible products to intangible feelings and attitudes, from dollar amounts to group cohesiveness and morale. When we think of performance results, however, we usually focus on quantifiable outcomes and overlook such intangibles as feelings and attitudes. Thus we ignore important results that build the foundation for the future and thereby deny ourselves opportunities for taking constructive action. For example, assume cohesion and morale in a group declines because it has been assigned the impossible task of producing 90 units per day. When the group fails to accomplish this task, each member blames the others, and the group falls apart. Management doesn't notice the group has disintegrated because they are too busy concentrating on the group's failure to produce 90 units a day. An easier goal is set for the group with the expectation they certainly should be able to handle it. By this time, however, the group has disintegrated so far it can't do anything productive.

Because the results of the present become the basis of performance in the future, the full range of expected results must be established and closely monitored. Management cannot be solely concerned with the quantity of goods produced—they have to be aware of what has happened to the materials and human resources in the production process. A high quantity of goods produced at present may also mean higher management expectations, depleted resources, and overflowing distribution channels in the future. A lower quantity of goods produced may result in backed-up resources, lack of employee development, reduced group cohesiveness, and low morale in the future.

An organization's objectives in this full range of desired results must be based on what will benefit the company as a whole and not on individual desires. We have all been in situations where people are working feverishly toward their own personal objectives, and no one really knows or cares what the organization is trying to accomplish. For example, an engineering group may get involved in designing highly complex bridges when what is really needed is landfill to control flooding and provide transportation. The problem, of course, is that the engineers know very little about landfill and a lot about bridges. If they don't know what the organization wants, naturally they choose an objective that matches their own skills and interests. Another example is the marketing representative who spends hours making a sales presentation to a potential customer when careful analysis would indicate that the cost of making the sale is more than the company can possibly recoup in profits. Since marketing representatives know how to develop sales presentations and may not understand or enjoy accounting and cost analysis, they will naturally tend to work toward their own sales objectives rather than take the organization's profit objective as their own.

Most of us spend years developing our skills and becoming specialized. We develop our own value systems and want to accomplish personal goals. Unfortunately we often become emotionally attached to our specialty and forget the objectives of the organization. We continue to do what we know, even though it may not be related to what the organization needs. An associate dean of a business school, after trying to get the various departments in his school to cooperate, recently referred to this as "hardening of the categories." "These people are like my kids," he lamented using an old saying, "You give them a hammer and it's amazing how many things in the house suddenly need hammering." The dean had a point; as soon as you receive a degree in a specialized area, amazingly all problems are suddenly finance problems, or accounting problems, or economic problems. (This is all quite peculiar, of course, because we all know that most organizational problems are really human problems and if the accountants and financial planners would just turn the world over to us social scientists, we could solve them all.)

This "hardening of the categories" is as much a fault of organizations as of specialists. Often the specialists don't know what the organization's objective are because no one has told them. They might be able to do what needs to be done fairly easily, if only they knew what the organization was trying to accomplish.

Modern technology and the highly complex techniques used in today's organizations demand very specialized knowledge, but specialization tends to narrow people's focus. Specialists in different fields think differently, act differently, and value different outcomes; this creates conflict when they get together. Because of the possibility of conflicting objectives, misunderstandings, and communication problems, specialists who work together have to make a special effort to explain their positions early, understand the positions of others, and resolve their differences in a way that will further the objectives of the organization.

The engineer's beautiful bridges are of little value if flood control is needed. The marketing representative's sales presentation is wasted if it results in sales not profitable to the organization. But the engineer and marketing representative won't realize this unless the organizational objectives are well defined and communicated. Only after defining the organization's goals can a manager rationally organize the work to be done. Without this, employees are left to pursue their own individual objectives.

Even with clear organization objectives, workers have many demands made on them. Supervisors expect certain results from their work on the job and directly influence those results through making requests, giving guidance, providing resources, giving rewards, etc. Supervisors are also involved in the formal programs of goal setting and performance appraisal that give them even more opportunities to influence their subordinates.

An employee's peers will also have expectations about what he or she should be doing on the job. Often peers are linked together in such a way that the performance of one person determines what the next person can do. Because they are interdependent, employees try to meet each others' needs. The more people an employee interacts with, the more demands he or she faces. These demands will often be more than the employee can handle. Sometimes demands of different persons or groups may be diametrically opposed to one another.

For example, an engineer in a manufacturing firm may interact with many people, each with a different set of demands. The production supervisor may want simple products, those that are easy to make and that don't change frequently. The sales manager might want something totally different; he or she deals directly with the customers and wants to be able to respond to their needs with many different products. Unlike the production supervisor, the sales manager will favor big inventories (so that the product is always immediately available), and high quality products at low prices. The accounting/finance department will place demands on the engineer that differ from the production supervisor or the sales manager. The accounting/finance department wants to keep costs down. They will favor low inventories to avoid finance charges. They will want the engineer to make standardized products that are cheap to make and very profitable.

Everyone who is dependent on the engineer will communicate his or her particular demands and expect to have them met. What makes the problem even worse is that the engineer will also have his or her own ideas about what needs to be done. The engineer may want to make very sophisticated, one-of-a-kind, state-of-the-art gadgets that are expensive, unprofitable, and hard to produce.

With differing demands and expectations being made upon them, employees will be confused. They have to sort out the many demands and establish objectives productive to the organization to which to devote their time and energy.

HOW ARE EXPECTATIONS ESTABLISHED AND COMMUNICATED?

Both supervisor and employee should sort out the many demands and establish performance expectations through a process of negotiating. Why negotiation? Many people think negotiation means that both parties have to make concessions and lose something in order to come to a compromise. Is that really necessary? Discussion is necessary, the understanding of the other party's perspectives is necessary, but neither party has to lose anything. Both gain something simply by clarifying their expectations so that their time and effort can be focused on the proper goal.

Often agreements can be made in such a way that both parties are winners. Negotiating not only improves understanding but increases the commitment of both the supervisor and worker to obtaining their goals because each is actively involved in defining objectives and developing realistic expectations.

Most organizational behavior theory is built on the assumption that people work well if they are treated with trust, openness, and understanding. It assumes that people are growth oriented and willing to accept personal responsibility for decisions and productivity. The dominant assumption is that people will be collaborative and productive if given enough freedom to make decisions. Another school of theorists, however, insist that competition, conflict, and the struggle to dominate are very real in organizations. The forces working on the employee aren't all benevolent and growth oriented; real conflicts exist that must be solved. When people have power over other people's actions, time, and resources, they don't hesitate to use it.

Considering expectations and goals as components of performance that need negotiating fits both sets of assumptions about the workplace. Negotiating assumes differences between the supervisor and employee exist and must be worked out. Everyone with whom the worker interacts has his or her own expectations. These expectations may be a result of power and conflict, different perceptions, or different positions. Whatever the source, differences and misunderstandings must be resolved before work will be productive.

The negotiating and problem-solving approaches to conflict resolution assume that each side will have input and be involved in determining the solution. Differences will be resolved so each party understands what the other is expected to do and accomplish. Motivation will be increased because both the employee and supervisor will be involved in and have some influence on the final decision; performance will be improved because time and effort will now be focused on agreed-on and carefully considered objectives rather than fragmented in the pursuit of unclear and unrealistic objectives.

Following are the various steps of negotiating and establishing performance expectations.

Step 1: Preliminary Planning

Before the supervisor and employee discuss performance expectations, initial plans for employee performance should be developed. In this step, both the supervisor and the employee should develop preliminary performance expectations that are stated as clearly and concretely as possible. These should be exchanged so that each party understands what the other expects. By comparing the two lists, both participants should be able to develop a list of problems and questions to be discussed.

The supervisor should be specific about the purpose of the discussion and what needs to be accomplished in it. He or she should then develop a plan for accomplishing this purpose based on an understanding of the other person. The more the manager knows about the employee, the better able he or she is to plan the discussion. The two main questions to be answered in preparation for the discussion are: (1) To what extent should the interview be planned and controlled and to what extent should it be free flowing? (2) What kinds of questions should be asked?

The manager will want to maintain a high degree of control in the discussion if the job involves very specific responsibilities. In this case, most of the questions to be addressed can be clearly identified in advance and there will not be much flexibility in the answers. The discussion is then a chance to communicate expectations that have already been established. If the responsibilities of the job are unclear, the discussion will be less structured and its flow will be determined by the problems that arise.

The questions to be asked will also be determined by the nature of the goals to be established. If the goals of the job have already been established, the purpose of the questions will be to make sure the goals are understood. If the goals of the job are unclear, the questions will be directed at defining them.

Step 2: Clarifying the Purpose of the Interview

Even though the interview is for the express purpose of establishing performance expectations, this purpose should be reviewed. Very often two parties will assume they understand the purpose of the discussion, but after 30 minutes of talking together, discover they do not agree at all. Better to repeat the obvious and make sure both parties agree.

Step 3: Preview of How the Interview Will Proceed

After the purpose of the meeting is clarified, the next step is to determine what topics you want to cover and how they should be discussed. The types of information needed for the discussion will have already been decided on in the preliminary planning. This is a chance to make sure the appropriate information is available and to decide how it should be used in the discussion. The two parties should also decide how they will relate to each other during the discussion. The person being interviewed needs to know what level of involvement is expected: Is he or she to help define the problem, solve the problem, or merely understand the problem and the solutions that have been developed?

This is also the time to lay out the sequence of the interview. If more information is needed, it should be collected before proceeding with the discussion. If problems need to be defined, that must be done before solutions are developed. The natural tendency of both participants will be to jump immediately to solutions, unless they clearly establish that the initial focus will be on defining the problem.

Step 4: Motivation and Involvement of the Subordinate

In order to define and communicate expectations effectively, subordinates must be involved; they need to help define the goals so they understand and are committed to attaining them.

Most subordinates will approach the discussion with some apprehension.

They will be unsure of what is to happen during the discussion and assume that since the manager is in a superior position, he or she should lead. The degree to which the manager dominates the discussion should be determined by the purpose of the discussion: if the purpose is to communicate previously established performance expectations, the superior will dominate; if the purpose is to help employees set their own goals, subordinates will dominate. To determine whether the interview has allowed the subordinate to become involved, we can calculate two ratios: questions to answers and listening to talking. Asking questions is the best way to involve the subordinate in the discussion. If the manager is continually asking questions, the employee will be naturally involved. If the manager spends most of the time giving answers, the subordinate has no opportunity to become involved. In that case, the only way the subordinate can become involved is to challenge the answers the manager is providing.

Asking questions is one way for managers to involve their subordinates in an interview. The other is listening. A question invites the employee to become involved, listening makes it possible for him or her to do so. If the supervisor wants the employee to become involved, he or she must make a conscious effort to listen.

Step 5: The Body of the Discussion

Performance problems are solved, misunderstandings cleared up, and new performance standards established in the body of the discussion. The sequence of topics discussed will be determined by the problems and opportunities discussed. The problems should be defined *before* considering possible solutions. Each party needs to understand the other's perception of the problems and opportunities before they can formulate concrete and realistic performance expectations.

Step 6: Summary of the Conclusions

By the end of the discussion, a great deal of information will have been exchanged. Some of the discussion will have been relevant, a fair amount will be irrelevant. So much will have been said the conclusions may be unclear. Therefore the discussion should end with a summary and a restatement of specific performance expectations. The employee and the manager may perceive the conclusions somewhat differently, and this is a chance for them to discover any misunderstandings and to clarify differences. Too often if the conclusions are not restated, differences remain that affect the work done afterward. Managers assume their employees will be doing one thing while the employees believe they should be doing something entirely different.

The summary should not be a one-sided affair. Whenever performance expectations are defined, both parties have responsibilities. The employee has work to do in order to meet organizational goals. The manager has work to do in order to help employees. Both sets of responsibilities should be summarized at the end of the interview.

PROBLEMS TO ANTICIPATE

Some of the predictable problems in discussing performance expectations can be avoided with proper planning. Most of the problems arise when communication is faulty and the participants are either unable to recognize them or unwilling to spend the time and energy needed to solve them. Three of the most common problems are differing perceptions, noninvolvement, and an unwillingness to understand the other person's viewpoint.

Differing Perceptions

Each participant brings his or her own background to the discussion. Because their past experiences and present positions are different, their perceptions of people and events will vary and these differences should be anticipated and managed. The discussion should be structured in such a way that it forces natural differences in perception to be recognized early, and the manager should ask questions designed to allow the employee to uncover and resolve them.

In order to resolve differences, the manager must plan the discussion before it takes place. He or she will want to consider very carefully the questions that will identify differences in perceptions and formulate a sequence of questions leading to their resolution.

Noninvolvement

If the discussion is one sided, with the manager doing all the talking and forcing everything in his or her direction, it is unlikely that the employee will be committed to solving performance problems and developing realistic performance expectations. Because involvement of the subordinate is critical to the success of the discussion, the manager's questions are extremely important. These questions should not only gather information but should encourage the employee to share his or her perceptions of the job, help define any problems that have arisen and participate in working out the solutions.

Lack of Understanding of the Other Person

Because we all have different experiences in life, understanding other's perspectives is hard. To the extent we don't understand other's positions, we will not be able to help them design realistic and challenging performance expectations.

The manager must look beyond the employee's words and understand the needs and experiences behind them. The statement, "I need more challenging opportunities" may mean "Let's raise the goal considerably," "I want to work with different people," "I would like to develop new skills" or "I'm leaving the organization." By understanding the person, we are better able to understand the statements he or she makes.

The need for understanding the person you'll be interviewing again emphasizes the importance of planning. You can't just rush into a discussion of performance. You need time to gather and analyze the kind of information necessary to make your discussion productive. By planning and managing the discussion carefully, realistic objectives can be set for both the employee and the manager. The key point to remember is that the performance discussion is a two-way process, and both the manager and employee should leave the discussion with a clear understanding of what the employee's goals are and what they both must do in order to accomplish them.

SUMMARY

An employee's understanding of his or her responsibilities is influenced from many sources. Supervisors, peers, acquaintances, and the environment all make demands on them. Sometimes these demands are complementary, sometimes conflicting. The worker has to combine these demands and decide what to accomplish.

What others expect of the worker is often determined by their position: supervisors expect performance, peers expect companionship, subordinates expect support and resources. Because of different expectations supervisors and employees must negotiate and establish clear objectives. For the manager, negotiating and establishing clear performance expectations involves six steps.

1. Plan the discussion.
2. Clarify the purpose of the discussion.
3. Preview the way the interview will proceed.
4. Motivate and involve the subordinate.
5. Manage the body of the discussion.
6. Summarize the conclusions.

Figure 6-1 is a questionnaire that can be used to analyze a discussion to determine if all of these steps have been included.

Analyzing the Performance Discussion

1. Clarification of purpose
   a. Was the purpose of the discussion made clear in the beginning?

   b. Was the problem to be addressed described in specific terms?

2. Preview of topics
   After the purpose of the discussion is clarified, the person being interviewed will usually be asking him or herself "What kind of information does my supervisor want?" Rather than guessing the answer to this question, it is best to lay out the topics initially and then suggest a way of talking about them.
   a. Was it clear what topics were to be discussed?

   b. Did the participants have a chance to talk about how to conduct the discussion?

3. Motivation of employee
   The person being interviewed must be actively involved in the discussion. His or her views and commitment to the problem-solving process is crucial. A good way to assess how well the interviewer involves the employee in the discussion is to consider the types of questions asked and how much listening the interviewer did.
   a. Did the interviewer ask relevant questions? Did the interviewer spend a lot of time trying to give answers and telling the other person what to do?

   b. Did the interviewer listen? Did the interviewer spend too much time talking?

Figure 6-1 Questionnaire for analyzing performance discussions.

c. Did the person interviewed have a chance to participate in defining the problem?

4. Body of the discussion
   a. Did the participants jump too quickly to a consideration of possible solutions before the problem was accurately described?

   b. Did the participants agree on what the problem was?

5. Summary
   a. Did the participants reach a conclusion?

   b. Did both participants leave with a clear understanding of what each was going to do to solve the problem, that is, did each have a plan of action?

   c. Did they set times for completing their tasks and getting back together? Were feedback mechanisms put in place?

SEVEN
SPECIFYING AND MANAGING ACTIVITIES

INTRODUCTION

Employees activities (i.e., how they spend their time and what they do) have a tremendous effect on what they accomplish. Activities are the behavioral manifestations of all the advance preparations: goal setting, discussions, directing, training, etc. Resources, technology, and human energy come together in activities and are translated into results. Managers and employees set goals, negotiate responsibilities, and obtain resources so that activities can be properly focused and produce desired results.

If the employees fail because their activities are misdirected and inappropriate, then all the preparation goes for naught. In previous chapters we talked about how management can affect the goals and expectations of employees. In this chapter we discuss how management can affect employees' activities.

Managers affect job activities by controlling the three factors of organizational performance:

1. By determining the *technology* used on the job.
2. By defining what responsibilities are included in the job and with whom the employee will work (its *structure*).
3. By controlling what and how *human resources* are used on the job.

Managing activities on the job begins with an analysis to determine the nature and characteristics of the job. Based on this analysis jobs can be designed or redesigned to maximize human performance. Managing activities thus consists of three steps: (1) analyzing the jobs, (2) changing the technology, structure, and/or human resources where necessary to encourage more productive activities, and (3) monitoring progress. Consider each of these steps in detail.

ANALYZING JOBS

Job analyses are used to determine what the content of a job is and what the person on the job does. A main purpose of job analysis is to construct job descriptions and job specifications that form the basis of many management activities in the organization. Job descriptions are one- or two-page explanations of the tasks, duties, responsibilities, relationships, time requirements, and technology of a job. Job specifications are summaries of the skills, abilities, knowledge, and qualifications necessary to perform well on the job. Figure 7-1 presents examples of a job description and job specifications for the job of personnel officer.

Once the job descriptions and job specifications have been established they become the basis of employee activity on the job. Change and communicate a new job description and specification and employee activities should change. Job descriptions and specifications also become the basis of many management activities.

1. Recruiting. If from the job descriptions and specifications employers know exactly the skills necessary to perform the job, and applicants know exactly what will be expected of them, the right people will more likely be recruited and hired for the job.
2. Training and development. Job descriptions and specifications identify the skills and experience employees will need to perform well on the job. These become the basis of training and development programs.
3. Testing and selecting. Understanding job content makes developing tests for selecting people easier and increases the chances that the right people will be selected for the jobs.
4. Performance appraisals. Job descriptions and specifications make performance appraisals job related. Descriptions of what is expected becomes the basis of appraising performance.
5. Compensation. Using job descriptions and specifications, compensation can be tied directly to job requirements and performance.

Before looking at various ways jobs can be analyzed, consider the differences between the objective characteristics of the job and how they are perceived by employers, managers, and others in the organization. This distinction is important because employees often react to their perceptions and understanding of the job and not the way it objectively exists or is understood by others. If differences exist between employees' perceptions and actual characteristics of the job, important questions about how the job should be designed will be raised: (1) How do changes in the objective job characteristics affect the employees' perceptions? (2) How do employees respond to their perceptions?

Job description

General description

Performs responsible administrative work managing personnel activities of a large state agency or institution. Work involves responsibility for the planning and administration of a personnel program which includes recruitment, examination, selection, evaluation, appointment, promotion, transfer, and recommended change of status of agency employees, and a system of communication for disseminating necessary information to workers. Works under general supervision, exercising initiative and independent judgment in the performance of assigned tasks.

Examples of work performed

Participates in overall planning and policy making to provide effective and uniform personnel services.

Communicates policy through organization levels by bulletin, meetings, and personal contact.

Interviews applicants, evaluates qualifications, classifies applications.

Recruits and screens applicants to fill vacancies and reviews applications of qualified persons.

Confers with supervisors on personnel matters, including placement problems, retention or release of probationary employees, transfers, demotions, and dismissals of permanent employees.

Supervises administration of tests.

Initiates personnel training activities and coordinates these activities with work of officials and supervisors.

Establishes effective service rating system, trains unit supervisors in making employee evaluations.

Maintains employee personnel files.

Supervises a group of employees directly and through subordinates.

Performs related work as assigned.

Job specification

General qualification requirements

Experience and training

Should have considerable experience in personnel administration.

Education

Graduation from a four-year college or university, with major work in education and personnel administration.

Knowledge, skills, and abilities

Considerable knowledge of principles and practices of personnel administration; selection and assignment of personnel; job evaluation.

Figure 7-1 Job description and specification for a personnel officer. (*Source:* U.S. Department of Labor, *Dictionary of Occupation Titles,* 4th ed., Washington, D.C., U.S. Government Printing Office, 1977.)

Differences in perception are to be expected. Employee needs and experiences affect their understanding of the job, particularly if they are highly trained in a specialized area. The more highly trained employees are, the more likely they are to adopt their own special interpretation of the work.

Research supports the contention that people's perceptions of their jobs vary considerably. Pepinsky and Pepinsky (1961) explain the advantages of becoming familiar with the way the employee sees the job.

> We can anticipate the necessity of distinguishing between the task as defined by (A) the actor to whom it was assigned and (B) by the setter who assigns it. . . . Therefore, we may define the task, in the latter view, as the confronting of an actor with a designated stimulus situation in which he is required to follow stipulated rules of procedure in responding to the situation, and in which he must attempt to satisfy specified criteria by which the success of his acts is judged. . . . The task setter is assumed to be operating for the social system, both in stipulating the actor's rules of procedure and in judging the extent to which the actor satisfies the task setter's criteria of success. This is called the official task—to distinguish it from the actor's private task or problem. Thus, the actor may or may not respond to the assigned official task as if it were a problem to him.

Viewed from the perspective of the employee, the job becomes whatever he or she defines it to be. The manager's view of the job, as communicated to the employees, is merely one of many sources of information they use to decide what to do and accomplish. Researchers and managers accepting this theory argue it is not the objective characteristics of the job people respond to but the task as they perceive it. Therefore, in order to understand and manage performance, the manager must understand the worker's perception of his or her job.

The problem created by recognizing differences in perceptions is that it introduces the whole range of human motivation into management's attempt to understand performance. In order to understand employee's perceptions the manager will have to understand each individual under his or her supervision. We cannot assume that the employee sees the world exactly the way we do. For example, in a study by Norman Maier and his associates (Maier, Hoffman, Hoover, and Reed, 1961) 58 pairs of managers and subordinates were asked questions about the work that the subordinates were supposed to be doing. Only 45 percent of the pairs gave matching answers to more than one-half of the questions about responsibilities on the job. Even more revealing was the fact that only 8 percent could agree on what would cause poor performance. Either the subordinates didn't know what was expected of them, or the managers really didn't know what the subordinate needed to do in order to perform well.

Undoubtedly numerous individual and organizational characteristics affect such conflicting perceptions. Baird and Mainstone (1975); Baird and Kim (1976) have found those who are involved with their work and committed to performing well on the job tend to report that their job has more positive characteristics than those who are not. Charns (1976) has found perceptions of a job varied with departmental membership and organizational levels.

Other than these and a few other limited studies, organizational research has generally not considered what causes variation in perception of jobs; we know, however, variation related to what the individual does on the job undoubtedly exists. To cope with these perceptual differences, managers should find out how employees view their jobs rather than assuming employees views agree with their own.

Approaches to Job Analysis

Techniques for analyzing jobs vary according to the following.

1. The forms and tools available to collect the information. The forms and tools available to analyze jobs vary from those that focus on objective characteristics to those that measure perceptions.
2. Who does the analysis. The analysis may be done by anyone: jobholder, supervisor, personnel specialist, independent observer, etc. Each approaches the job from a different perspective and will provide different but equally important analyses.

Consider the more objective approaches to job analysis first, then those that focus on perceptions. Remember the more subjective the form or tool, the more the analysis is likely to vary according to who is doing the rating. Time and motion studies are the most objective approach and vary little according to who is doing the analysis. Interviews are the most subjective and will sometimes vary widely depending on who is doing the interview.

Time and Motion Studies

Time and motion studies are the most objective of job analysis techniques and involve standardized methods and provide quantified results that can be easily compared. Time studies strive to define "the time needed by a qualified operator to perform the operation while working at a normal pace" (Brief and Aldag, 1978). The standard time for completing a job as specified is then used to schedule work, set wages, establish training programs, etc.

Motion studies focus on determining ways to do a job that will minimize cost and effort. What are the basic motions needed to produce results? Motion studies often involve a flowchart, which provides an overall picture of the steps from the beginning to the end of the job. Figure 7-2 gives examples of the symbols commonly used in motion studies. Time and motion studies are the most objective of the job analysis techniques. They provide accurate descriptions of what a person does on the job. Time and motion studies do not account for the cognitive and interpersonal aspects of the job, however.

Symbol	Symbol Name	Description
O	Operation	A change in an item, such as in size or shape, occurs.
⇨	Transportation	An item or individual moves from one workplace to another.
D	Delay	An item or individual must wait.
△	Storage	A controlled storage condition exists in which an order is needed to take the item out of storage and move it to the next scheduled activity.
□	Inspection	An item is compared to some standard.

Figure 7-2 Symbols used in motion studies. (*Source:* R. J. Aldag and A. P. Brief, *Task Design and Employee Motivation,* Scott, Foresman and Company, Glenview, Ill., 1979, p. 71.)

Functional Job Analysis

Fine and his associates developed functional job analysis providing a concrete method of analyzing physical, cognitive and interpersonal activities on the job (Fine and Wiley, 1974). Their methodology sees jobs as broken down into many tasks. "Tasks" are defined as "an action or action sequence grouped through time, designed to contribute to the accomplishment of an objective and for which functional levels and orientations can be reliably assigned." They see the action process as oriented towards either things or physical activities, such as operating a typewriter; information or mental activities, such as analyzing data; or people and interpersonal activities, such as consulting with another person. In addition to the orientation of the activities, functional job analysis identifies in uniform job descriptions the levels of complexity associated with each of the orientations. Fine and Wiley (1974) offer the following descriptions of functional job analysis (FJA).

> What FJA does is provide (1) a standardized, controlled language to describe *what workers do* and (2) a means of assessing and measuring the *level* and *orientation* of what workers do. As a tool for controlling the language of tasks and measuring their complexity, FJA can be described in terms of the following principles:
>
> 1. What workers do as they perform the tasks that make up their jobs, they do in relation to Data, People, and Things. All jobs involve the workers, to some extent, with information or ideas (Data), with clients or co-workers (People), and with machines or equipment (Things). Workers function in unique ways

in each of these areas. For example, when a worker's task involves him with machines or equipment (Things), the worker draws upon his physical resources (strength, dexterity, motor coordination, and so forth). When a worker's task involves him with information or ideas (Data), the worker calls his mental resources into play (knowledge, thought, intuition, insight, and so forth). When a worker's task involves him with clients, customers, and co-workers (People), the worker draws upon his interpersonal resources (empathy, courtesy, warmth, openness, guile, and so forth). All jobs require the worker to relate to each of these areas and in doing so require him to draw upon his resources in each of these areas to some degree.

2. The concrete and specific actions workers perform in relation to Data, People, and Things as they execute different tasks can probably be described in an infinite number of ways; that is, there are as many specific ways of expressing what workers do in relation to Data, People, and Things as there are specific tasks to be performed or unique content and conditions to which to relate. While there may be an infinite number of ways of describing tasks, there is only a handful of significant patterns of behavior (functions) which describe how workers use themselves in relation to Data, People, and Things. Those patterns of behavior which can be articulated reliably have been defined in *Worker Function Scales,* (see Figure 7-3) the primary tools of FJA, which provide a standardized, controlled language to describe what workers do in the entire universe of work.

   For example, in relation to information and ideas, a worker functions to *compare, compile, compute,* or *analyze* data.

   In interacting with clients, customers, and co-workers, workers *serve, exchange information, coach,* or *consult* with people.

   In using equipment, workers *feed, tend, operate,* or *set up* machines and *drive/control* vehicles.

   Although each of these worker functions is performed under widely varying conditions, occurs over a range of difficulty, and involves different specific content, each, within its scope, calls for similar kinds and degrees of worker characteristics to achieve effective performance.

3. The functions in each of the three areas of Data, People, and Things can be defined by a Worker Function Scale, in which the performance requirements range from the simple to the complex in an ordinal scale (See Appendix for an example of one of these scales, the Data Function Scale.). Because the scale is ordinal (that is, one in which any point on the scale includes lower levels and excludes higher levels), the selection of a specific function to reflect the requirements of a particular task indicates that the task includes the lower functions and excludes the higher ones. For example, on scanning the Worker Function Scale for Data, when one selects the *compiling* function as the appropriate worker behavior to describe the way a worker must relate to information in a given task, he is deciding two things: (1) that the worker's performance is more complex than *copying* and less complex than *analyzing;* and (2) that the worker must be able to perform all or at least comprehend all the data functions below *compiling,* but does not have to be able to perform or comprehend higher functions such as *analyzing* or *coordinating.*

4. The three hierarchies of Data, People, and Things functions provide two

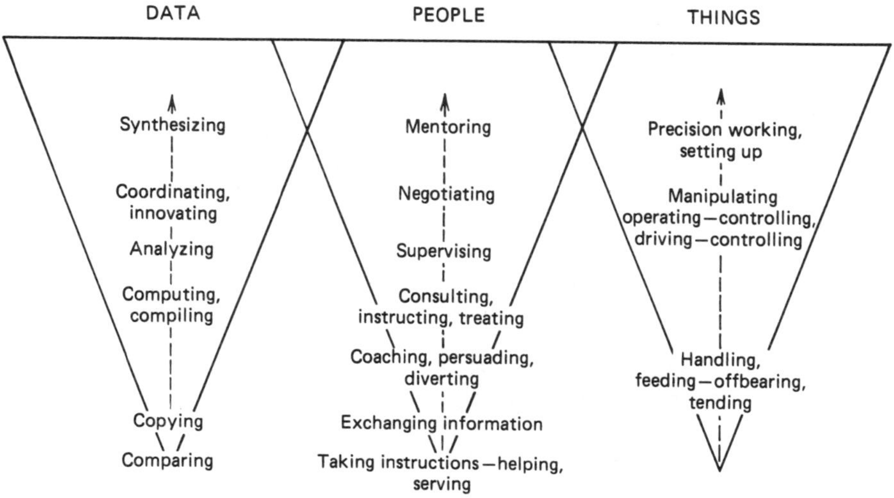

Figure 7-3 Summary chart of worker function scales. Each successive function reading down usually or typically involves all those that follow it. The functions separated by a comma are separate functions on the same level separately defined. They are on the same level because empirical evidence does not make a hierarchical distinction clear. The hyphenated functions *Taking Instructions-Helping, Operating-Controlling, Driving-Controlling,* and *Feeding-Offbearing* are single functions. *Setting Up, Operating-Controlling, Driving-Controlling, Feeding-Offbearing,* and *Tending* are special cases involving machines and equipment of *Precision Working, Manipulating,* and *Handling,* respectively, and hence are indented under them. (*Source:* From S. Fine and W. Wiley, "An Introduction to Functional Job Analysis," in E. Fleishman and A. Bass (eds.), *Studies in Personnel and Industrial Psychology,* 3rd ed., The Dorsey Press, Homewood, Ill., 1974.)

ways of systematically comparing and measuring the requirements of any task in any job. These two measures are *level* and *orientation.* The *level* measure indicates the relative complexity or simplicity of a task when it is compared to other tasks. The level is expressed by selecting the function that best describes the pattern of behavior in which the worker engages to perform a given task effectively. The ordinal position of the function is the level measure. For example, to say that a worker in dealing with the Data content of a task is *compiling,* one has indicated that he is functioning at level 3B on the Data scale, which requires a higher level of functioning than is required in *copying* information (level 2) but is a lower level of functioning than *analyzing data* (level 4).

The *orientation* measure provided by FJA indicates the relative involvement of the worker with Data, People, and Things as he performs a given task. A basic concept of FJA is that the worker is not equally involved with all three in any task and that his relative involvement with any of the three may change from task to task. For example, in performing one task in his job, a worker may be involved almost exclusively with Data; that is, something like 75 percent of his involvement, and the resources he draws upon to perform a task are related to Data at the *compiling* level; but in order to accomplish the task, he must also be involved interpersonally in *exchanging information* with co-workers (perhaps 15 percent) as well as in calling upon physical resources in *handling* various documents, paper, and pen (10 percent). The worker's total functional involvement with Data (75 percent), People (15 percent), and Things (10 percent) adds up to 100 percent.

The orientation measure, then, is expressed by assigning a percentage in units of five or ten to each of the three functions so that the total adds up to 100 percent. Note that these percentages are estimates. The reliability sought is in the pattern of the three estimates, not in the absolute amount of the estimates.

The orientation measure is a reflection of the performance requirements of a task. In the example above the estimates assigned must be in accord with the independent judgment that this task will be evaluated overwhelmingly on its data standards and quite lightly with regard to its people and things standards. The training the worker must have to perform the task should emphasize and build the mental skills required. The supervisor's instructions to the worker should emphasize and reflect the nature of the mental performance expected and the data standards by which the worker's results will be judged.

5. With the assignment to a given task of these two measures—level and orientation—the worker's total involvement with the specific content of his tasks—mentally, physically, and interpersonally—is obtained. Level and orientation are determined by selecting three functions, one from each of the three scales, most characteristic of the requirements of each task (yielding *level* measures). Each function is then weighted to show how much emphasis falls upon its requirements in the performance of the task (yielding *orientation* measures).

   For the task example used previously,

6. Since the level and orientation measures can be applied to all tasks and, by integration, to all jobs, the Worker Function Scales provide a means for comparing all tasks and all jobs on a common basis. This, of course, is a step forward from the situation where tasks cannot be compared because of the infinite number of ways of describing specific content.

APPENDIX

Complete Version of Data Function Scale

The arabic numbers assigned to definitions represent the successive levels of this ordinal scale. The *A* and *B* definitions are variations on the same level. There is no ordinal difference between *A* and *B* definitions on a given level.

Level	Definition
1	Comparing—Selects, sorts, or arranges data, people, or things, judging whether their readily observable functional, structural, or compositional characteristics are similar to or different from prescribed standards.
2	Copying—Transcribes, enters, and/or posts data, following a schema or plan to assemble or make things and using a variety of work aids.
3A	Computing—Performs arithmetic operations and makes reports and/or carries out a prescribed action in relation to them.
3B	Compiling—Gathers, collates, or classifies information about data, people, or things, following a schema or system but using discretion in application.
4	Analyzing—Examines and evaluates data (about things, data, or people) with reference to the criteria, standards, and/or requirements of a particular discipline, art, technique, or craft to determine interaction effects (consequences) and to consider alternatives.
5A	Innovating—Modifies, alters, and/or adapts existing designs, procedures, or methods to meet unique specifications, unusual conditions, or specific standards of effectiveness within the overall framework of operating theories, principles, and/or organizational contexts.
5B	Coordinating—Decides time, place, and sequence of operations of a process, system, or organization, and/or the need for revision of goals, policies (boundary conditions), or procedures on the basis of analysis of data and of performance review of pertinent objectives and requirements. Includes overseeing and/or executing decisions and/or reporting on events.
6	Synthesizing—Takes off in new directions on the basis of personal intuitions, feelings, and ideas (with or without regard for tradition, experience, and existing parameters) to conceive new approaches to or statements of problems and the development of system, operational, or aesthetic "solutions" or "resolutions" of them, typically outside of existing theoretical, stylistic, or organizational context.

An outgrowth of functional job analysis is the *Dictionary of Occupational Titles*. First compiled by the United States Employment Service in 1939, the latest edition of the *Dictionary of Occupational Titles (DOT)* contains almost 40,000 titles and almost 25,000 comprehensive job descriptions. See Figure 7-4 for the DOT description of a job analyst.

The *DOT* classification system is done with a numerical coding system, based on three sets of numbers. The first set illustrates occupational categories, the first digit representing the broad occupational group, the second digit the division within the group, and the third digit the group within the division. For example, the job analyst with a code of 166.267-018,

166.267-018—JOB ANALYST (profess. & kin.) personnel analyst
Collects, analyzes, and prepares occupational information to facilitate personnel, administration, and management functions of organization: Consults with management to determine type, scope, and purpose of study. Studies current organizational occupational data and compiles distribution reports, organization and flowcharts, and other background information required for study. Observes jobs and interviews workers and supervisory personnel to determine job and worker requirements. Analyzes occupational data, such as physical, mental, and training requirements of jobs and workers and develops written summaries, such as job descriptions, job specifications and lines of career movement. Utilizes developed occupational data to evaluate or improve methods and techniques for recruiting, selecting, promoting, evaluating, and training workers and administration of related personnel programs. May specialize in classifying positions according to regulated guidelines to meet job classification requirements of civil service system and be known as POSITION CLASSIFIER (gov. ser.).

Figure 7-4 Job description for a job analyst. (*Source:* U.S. Department of Labor, Employment and Training Administration, *Dictionary of Occupational Titles,* 4th ed., Washington, D.C., U.S. Government Printing Office, 1977, pp. 99–100.)

according to the *DOT,* is a (1) professional, in (6) administrative specializations, in (6) personnel administration.

The middle set of the nine-digit code illustrates the worker function ratings, with respect to the data, people, and things divisions of the functional job analysis. Numbers decrease with difficulty of the task. Thus, the job analyst (2) analyzes data as opposed to comparing it, (6) exchanges information or signals and speaks to people as opposed to supervising, and (7) handles things, as opposed to operating/controlling them.

The last set of digits indicates the occupations, alphabetically by title, which are of the same occupational group—that is, those having the same first three digits. The numbers "010" would indicate that there are no other occupations in the same group. Job analysts, therefore, are only one of several other occupations within the "166" group because the last three digits are "018."

The *DOT,* a national publication, increases uniformity in titles, descriptions, and hiring policies making comparisons of jobs easier. Compensation, equity, transfers, training, and promotions across jobs are possible because the DOT provides this way of comparing jobs.

Quantitative Job Analysis (QJA)

Functional job analysis (FJA), largely because of its descriptive, somewhat subjective nature, has come under criticism. Some feel the descriptions attempt to cover too wide of job range. As a result, each description is general, and applies to no single specific job very accurately. Also, since the methodology is complex, the analysts must be skilled at translating performances, functions, outputs and job contents into valid descriptions. Quantitative job analysis (QJA) are essentially detailed, quantifiable extensions of

FJA created to reduce these problems. QJA are lengthy, specific assessments of the tasks and worker traits involved in a job that are more systematic and less subject to error than the FJA. However, they are more costly and time consuming to develop and implement.

QJA operates on the basis of a task/trait inventory, a questionnaire that lists all the aspects of work to be analyzed. The tasks are usually measured in terms of their importance and training and accomplishment times. Traits such as knowledge, skills, and abilities are measured in terms of their importance and prior experience necessary to attain them. An example of QJA is the Position Analysis Questionnaire (PAQ) (Figure 7-5).

Position Analysis Questionnaire

The Position Analysis Questionnaire (PAQ) developed by McCormick and his associates (McCormick, Jeanneret, and Mecham, 1969) is the most widely used method of quantitative job analysis. The PAQ method assumes jobs are composed of a common set of behavioral building blocks. Once these

Information Input (35)

Sources of job information (20): Use of written materials
Discrimination and perceptual activities (15): Estimating speed of moving objects

Mediation Processes (14)

Decisions making and reasoning (2): Reasoning in problem solving
Information processing (6): Encoding, decoding
Use of stored information (6): Using mathematics

Work Output

Use of physical devices (29): Use of keyboard devices
Integrative manual activities (8): Handling objects, materials
General body activities (7): Climbing
Manipulation, coordination (8): Level of supervision received

Interpersonal Activities

Communications; interpersonal relationships; personal contact; supervision and coordination

Work Situation and Job Context (18)

Physical working conditions (12): Low temperature
Psychological and sociological aspects (6): Civic obligations

Miscellaneous Aspects (36)

Work schedule, method of pay, and apparel (21): Irregular hours
Job demands (12): Specified (controlled) work pace
Responsibility (3): Responsibility for safety of others

Figure 7-5 PAQ divisions, subdivisions, and specific examples. The numbers in parentheses refer to the number of items included in the questionnaire related to that category. For most of the job elements, the observer rates the job on a point scale ranging from "does not apply" to "highly applicable." (*Source:* E. J. McCormick, P. R. J. Jeanneret, and R. C. Mecham, "A Study of Job Characteristics and Job Dimensions as Based on the Position Analysis Questionnaire (PAQ)," *Journal of Applied Psychology Monograph,* 56, 1972, pp. 347–368.)

sets are identified, it is possible to describe jobs according to the degree to which they involve certain tasks.

In constructing the list of common components, McCormick's objective was to create a list of job elements that were (1) identifiable, (2) specific enough to be applied across a wide range of jobs, and (3) complete enough to characterize any job. In constructing this list, he focused on worker-oriented elements of jobs—the behaviors involved in doing them. These behaviors (examples of which are included in Figure 7-5) related to information input, mediation processes, work output, interpersonal activities, and behavioral "adjustments" to the job environment. The list developed can be used to describe any job.

The PAQ is the most widely used method of QJA, and the most available checklisting technique. The PAQ allows comparisons within a large and growing range of jobs but tends to focus only on similarities and is lengthy and time consuming.

Functional Job Attributes

Turner and Lawrence (1965) developed a conceptual framework focusing on job characteristics that have an affect on the attitudes and behaviors of employees. They identified three elements of behavior: activities—what people do, interactions—contact between people, and mental states—attitudes, feelings, cognitions, etc. Using these three elements of behavior, Turner and Lawrence identify six task attributes important for positive attitude and good performance: (1) variety—the number of different types of activities prescribed by the job, (2) autonomy—the amount of discretion the employee has over his or her activities, (3) required interaction—the amount of personal interaction necessary, (4) optional interaction—the amount of voluntary interaction feasible, (5) knowledge and skill required—the amount and complexity of knowledge and skill necessary to perform the job, and (6) responsibility—the degree of accountability involved.

Turner and Lawrence also specified six Associated Task Attributes (ATA): (1) task identity, (2) pay, (3) working conditions, (4) cycle time, (5) level of mechanization, and (6) capital investment. Figure 7-6 lists the indexes for measuring both the Requisite Task Attributes (RTA) and the ATA. Their method provides a good way to look at both objective characteristics of a job, such as average pay and amount of light, and also subjective characteristics, such as variety of work pace, and latitude in choice of work method.

Questionnaires and Interviews

PAQs is a structured checklisting method of data collection that provides structure and some objectivity to job analyses. Other more subjective methods include questionnaires, interviews, observations, supervisory conferences, critical incidents, and sampling as follows.

1. Questionnaires and interviews: rely on the jobholder to provide accurate descriptions of their responsibilities and functions. While structured checklists already contain all of the information to be analyzed and only ask for the importance of levels at which each item is performed, questionnaires and interviews are more subjective.

   An example of a questionnaire approach to job analysis is Hackman and Oldham's JOB Diagnostic Survey (JDS) (Hackman and Oldham, 1975). They used Turner and Lawrence's list as the basis for developing a set of perceived task characteristics at the core of human motivation and performance. Hackman and Oldham defined these core characteristics as: (1) variety, (2) autonomy, (3) task identity (the extent to which employees do a clearly defined portion of the work and can see the results of their efforts), (4) feedback, (5) dealing with others, and (6) friendship opportunities. These task characteristics are measured by having the employees or an observer fill out a questionnaire; Figure 7-7 provides an example of the types of questions used.

   The interview is a well-known subjective approach to job analysis. Cascio (1980) states that the interview is the most commonly used technique for establishing the tasks, duties, and behaviors of jobs. The worker who naturally has high detailed knowledge of the job can provide a good description. The success of interviews obviously rests on the skill of the interviewer.
2. Observations: performed by trained analysts provide information about specific sequences of behavior. Observations are best used to study repetitive, manual behaviors over short time periods where abstract reasoning will have little effect on results. Unlike questionnaires and interviews, the success of this approach rests with the accuracy of the observer's recordings, not the actual employee's report.
3. Supervisory conferences: in which an analyst guides the discussion and analyzes the information to determine the behaviors or personal skills/qualifications necessary for the execution of a specific task. Success here also is dependent on the expertise of the analyst.
4. Critical incidents: of behaviors that resulted in or contributed to particularly successful or unsuccessful job performance. Behaviors are recorded by supervisors, thus the validity of the information depends highly on them, instead of the employees or analysts.
5. Sampling: by diary, film, observation, or other periodic reporting techniques of a proportion of behaviors. This can be done cross sectionally, reporting for several different jobholders in one time frame, or longitudinally, reporting for one or two jobholders once a week or once a month over a specific time frame. Validity of the data depends on the collector and the collection method.

ACTIVITY
Object Variety
The number of parts, tools, and controls to be manipulated
Motor Variety—average of:
Variety in prescribed work place
Variety in physical location of work
Variety of prescribed physical operations of work
Autonomy—average of:
Amount of worker latitude in selection of work methods
Amount of worker latitude in selection of work sequences
Amount of worker latitude in selection of work pace
Amount of worker latitude in accepting or rejecting the quality of incoming materials
Amount of worker in securing outside services
INTERACTION
Required Interaction—average of:
Number of people required to interact with, at least every two hours
Quantity of time spent in required interactions
Optional Interaction on the Job—average of:
Number of people available for interaction in working area
Quantity of time available for interaction while working
Optional Interaction Off the Job
Amount of time worker is free to choose to leave the work area without reprimand
MENTAL STATES
Knowledge and Skill
Amount of time required to learn to perform job proficiently
Responsibility—average of:
Ambiguity of remedial action (to correct routine job problems)
Time span of discretion—(maximum time before marginal substandard work is detected)
Probability of serious (harmful or costly) error
ASSOCIATED TASK ATTRIBUTES
Task Identity—average of:
Clarity of cycle closure
Visibility of transformation (performed by the worker)
Visibility (of work transformation) in the finished product
Magnitude of (value added by the) transformation
Pay
Average weekly gross pay without overtime adjusted for U.S. and Canadian differential
Working Conditions—average of:
Amount of light and cleanliness in general work area
Amount of fumes, etc.
Temperature
Amount of dirt, grease, oil in immediate job area
Cycle Time
Length in time of major work cycle
Level of Mechanization
Jobs ranked by the technical sophistication of the machinery used
Capital Investment
Jobs ranked by estimated amount of capital invested per worker

Listed below are a number of statements which could be used to describe a job. You are to indicate whether each statement is an *accurate* or an *inaccurate* description of *your* job.
Once again, please try to be as objective as you can in deciding how accurately each statement describes your job—regardless of whether you like or dislike your job.

Write a number in the blank beside each statement, based on the following scale:

How accurate is the statement in describing your job?

1	2	3	4	5	6	7
Very Inaccurate	Mostly Inaccurate	Slightly Inaccurate	Uncertain	Slightly Accurate	Mostly Accurate	Very Accurate

________ **1.** The job requires me to use a number of complex or high-level skills.
________ **2.** The job requires a lot of cooperative work with other people.
________ **3.** The job is arranged so that I do *not* have the chance to do an entire piece of work from beginning to end.
________ **4.** Just doing the work required by the job provides many chances for me to figure out how well I am doing.
________ **5.** The job is quite simple and repetitive.
________ **6.** The job can be done adequately by a person working alone—without talking or checking with other people.
________ **7.** The supervisors and co-workers on this job almost *never* give me any "feedback" about how well I am doing in my work.
________ **8.** This job is one where a lot of other people can be affected by how well the work gets done.
________ **9.** The job denies me any chance to use my personal initiative or judgment in carrying out the work.
________ **10.** Supervisors often let me know how well they think I am performing the job.
________ **11.** The job provides me the chance to completely finish the pieces of work I begin.
________ **12.** The job itself provides very few clues about whether or not I am performing well.
________ **13.** The job gives me considerable opportunity for independence and freedom in how I do the work.
________ **14.** The job itself is *not* very significant or important in the broader scheme of things.

Figure 7-7 Questions used in Job Diagnostic Survey to measure task characteristics. (*Source:* J. R. Hackman and G. R. Oldham, *Work Redesign,* © 1980, Addison-Wesley, Reading, Mass., pp. 280–281.) Reprinted with permission.

Which Approach to Analyzing the Job Should You Use?

You should use the approach to job analysis that best fits your purpose and the type of job to be analyzed. The following are some broad guidelines for choosing among the alternatives.

Figure 7-6 (*opposite*) Indexes for measuring Requisite Task Attributes (RTA). (*Source:* Adapted from Turner, A. N., and Lawrence, P. R. *Industrial Jobs and the Worker,* Cambridge: Harvard University Graduate School of Business Administration, 1965, by Aldag, R. J. and Brief, A. P. *Task Design and Employee Motivation,* Scott Foresman and Company, Glenview, Illinois, 1979, pp. 48–49.)

1. *Determine How Observable the Job Is.* Some jobs naturally lend themselves to observation. In these cases, the more structured checklists and analysis procedures such as the PAQ or FJA are appropriate. If the job involves more mental rather than physical tasks or is always changing, a more probing analysis such as an interview will be needed.
2. *Recognize That the Person Who Does the Analysis Will Affect the Results.* While interviewing is a very subjective technique and can therefore produce widely varying results, such objective methods as Functional Job Analysis and the Position Analysis Questionnaire will also yield information that varies according to the person using them. Knowing who does the analysis and what perspective they have is important. Whenever possible, you should have both the jobholder's and a second party's evaluation of a job. Then you can determine whether the worker perceives the work the same way others do and how his or her perceptions correlate with performance on the job.
3. *Use a Procedure(s) That Can Be Understood by and Be Useful to Both Employees and Managers.* The purpose of job analysis is to provide a basis for manager and employee to work together to accomplish the organization's objectives. This can best happen when both understand the job.
4. *Remember That the Purpose of the Analysis Is to Describe Those Activities and Job Characteristics That Relate to Performance.* The method of analysis should be consistent with the nature of the job's performance requirements. If the job focuses on results, the analysis should focus on results; if the job deals primarily with behaviors, the analysis should deal with behaviors; if the job involves skills or resources, the analysis should focus on those elements.

CHANGING THE TECHNOLOGY, STRUCTURE, AND/OR HUMAN RESOURCES TO ENCOURAGE MORE PRODUCTIVE ACTIVITIES

If the activities on the job as identified by the job analysis are not producing the desired results, the activities should be changed. However, activities are not changed directly. They are adjusted by changing the three factors of organizational performance: technology, structure, and human resources.

Technology

Technology often has direct and immediate effect on job activities. It determines how work is done and who the employee will work with. Thompson (1967) proposed a useful model for analyzing the effect of technology on activities. He identified three types of technologies: long linked, mediating, and intensive.

Long-linked technologies are characterized by sequential relationships. The technology of one job extends into the next job. A classic example is the production line. Here the technology links the jobs together. Who the employee interacts with will be determined by what the technology requires to be done before and after the job. In fact, because the jobs are so closely linked by the technology, activities of one job cannot be changed without considering how it will affect and be affected by the other jobs. This type of technology creates a domino affect. If one part breaks down, the whole system goes. The activities in these jobs can be changed only by changing the jobs it is linked to.

Mediating technologies can best be characterized as coordinating systems. For instance, banks coordinate the needs of many savers and lenders, telephone companies coordinate offices, businesses, homes, recreation facilities, etc. Such organizations are like giant octopuses, reaching out to their scattered subunits. In this kind of technology, activities will vary depending on what is used to coordinate the jobs be it computers, phones, the mail, banks, or other services. Employees working with mediating technologies have to engage in those activities that coordinate the organization's subunits. Activities in these jobs can be changed only by changing the way the jobs are coordinated. For example, as banks have gradually shifted from paper and pencil recording of transactions to on-line computer and electronic recording, the nature of the job activities in banks has changed substantially.

Another characteristic of mediating technologies is standardization. For instance, banks work because everyone uses the same procedures. Bank employees spend a good deal of their time on the job entering information from customers onto standard forms to make sure it fits into the network. Changes in the activities of these jobs will happen when the way to coordinate and standardize the activities are changed.

Mediating technologies are also characterized by an inherent need to grow by adding on more subunits, for instance, banks become more powerful when they have a broader customer base. A company like United Parcel Service (UPS) becomes more successful by delivering to a greater number of destinations, and the telephone company endeavors to reach as many customers as possible. Thus, in organizations with mediating technologies, part of the employees' activities will be devoted to expanding the customer base. The nature of these activities will change as the nature of the customer base changes.

Intensive technologies work on a customer or project basis. Few standard procedures exist because everything must be flexible enough to adjust to the needs of the project. Rather than one set technology, there will be many options. The employees will be responsible for choosing the technology that best fits the job. Hospitals and research and development units are examples of organizations that use this type of technology. The employee must first analyze the client or project to determine which of the available technologies to use; their jobs will be characterized by activities associated with searching, analyzing, and planning. In intensive technologies, employees activities change in response to changes in their current client or product.

Each of these technologies has an unique way of affecting job activities and each limits the employee's options in different ways. Long-linked technologies place jobs in sequence so that the activities of each are determined by what happens before and after. Mediating technologies demand standardization and an ever-expanding customer base; activities are constrained by whatever the standard product is and by the method used to coordinate the organization's subunits. Intensive technologies must adapt to the customer; the employees' activities will depend on the customer being served.

Structure

We have defined structure as the responsibilities of the job in addition to the relationship of the jobholder to others in the organization. Using this definition, structure affects activities two ways. First, directly, by specifying the goals and responsibilities of the job. Second, indirectly by determining relationships with others.

We will not spend extensive time discussing how to affect activities through structure because it involves defining and communicating performance expectations described in Chapter Four and establishing and communicating the job description explained in this chapter. By way of review, remember that when you change the performance expectations, employees activities should change. Also, communicate a change in the description of the job and employees' activities should change. Job analyses identify the activities on a job. The job descriptions and specifications that result from the analyses establish activities and responsibilities for the employee. Establishing responsibilities and describing activities on the job are the most direct and powerful way of managing activities.

In general, the effect that relations with others has on employees activities will be determined by how dependent the job is on others in the organization. A person who depends on others to provide resources and assistance will be greatly affected by them. Similarly, if those who are consuming what the employee produces have strict specifications as to what they will accept, the activities of the employee will be greatly affected. The employees will have to produce exactly what the other person wants. Activities on the job will have to fit the needs of others. As these needs change the employees activities will change.

Human Resources

The third factor influencing employee activities is human resources. How are the personal characteristics of employees related to their activities on the job? Behavioral, cognitive, and skill theorists all seek answers to this question. Behavioral theorists suggest that people engage in activities that are rewarding. The questions behaviorists ask when analyzing activities on the job are: (1) What do people find rewarding? (2) What activities does the job reward? Cognitive theorists say that workers will engage in those activities they think are most likely to satisfy their needs. The questions they ask in analyzing activities are: (1) What needs do people have? (2) How do the activities fill those needs? (3) What expectations do people have? (4) How do the activities fulfill their expectations? Skill theorists don't focus on what people want to do but what they can do. The important questions for them are: (1) What abilities do the activities require? (2) How do people with various abilities respond to the performance requirements?

We have reviewed each of these theoretical approaches elsewhere, so they should be familiar to you. What we need to do now is consider them from the vantage point of job activities. These three theoretical approaches suggest three questions that can be useful in understanding job activities from the perspective of the person on the job.

1. What rewards are available from the job activities?
2. What do employees believe they are expected to do on the job?
3. What skills does the job require?

What Rewards Are Available from the Job Activities? Not only can we receive rewards for accomplishments on jobs; jobs can be rewarding in and of themselves. Some things are just fun to do. Activities enabling us to use skills and abilities we value are particularly rewarding. Social workers enjoy working with people, farm workers enjoy working outdoors, researchers in the physical sciences enjoy the experimentation that is part of their job. To make job activities more rewarding, we need to match the job requirements with the skills and abilities of the employee. If employees value their skills, they will enjoy using and developing them.

Lawler (1969) defines satisfaction from the work itself as intrinsic satisfaction and suggests that workers have these feelings when they *learn* that as a *result* of *their own efforts* they have *accomplished something worthwhile.*

Based on Lawler's definition, a set of job characteristics that will cause employees to have a sense of satisfaction and accomplishment when they perform well can be identified.

1. Skill variety—activities that challenge the person's skills and abilities.
2. Identity—completion of a whole and identifiable piece of work.

3. Significance—importance of the activity to others.
4. Autonomy—employee's freedom of action on the job.
5. Feedback—employee knowledge of his or her accomplishment relative to organizational goals.

When these characteristics are present in jobs, workers are able to give themselves feelings of satisfaction. Further satisfaction comes when they accomplish organizational objectives. Activities are changed by changing the feelings of satisfaction employees give themselves and the rewards they receive for accomplishments. This is done by managing (1) the characteristics of the task—variety, identity, significance, autonomy, and feedback and (2) external rewards.

What Do Employees Believe They Are Expected to Do on the Job? Employees do what they think they are expected to do. These expectations are based on information they receive from those they work with and from other sources in and out of the organization. Often these expectations conflict, and then the employee must somehow reconcile all of these expectations and decide on a feasible course of action. The natural tendency will be for the employee to interpret these expectations from his or her own vantage point. For example, a supervisor might ask an employee in marketing to develop an ad campaign for a new type of paint. The employee, being highly trained in quantitative analysis, develops a massive research project to determine competitive position, customer preferences, and mass media strategy. He or she then writes a report recommending product characteristics, distribution channels, packaging, and price when all the time what the supervisor, who comes from an art background, wanted was a billboard layout. Activities on the job are best explained by considering how the employee interprets the job. If activities are to be changed, the employees' expectations will need to be revised by establishing and communicating the new expectations.

What Skills Does the Job Require? As in the foregoing example, the activities and skills of employees have a circular relationship. People will tend to use the skills they have; thus skills influence the activities the employee will engage in. Similarly, the activities people engage in determine the skills they have. The best way to determine how the activities and skills are related is to consider the skills the employee brought to the job and then what he/she learned while on the job.

As the performance audit presented in Chapter Three shows, because of the complex relationships that exist among technology, structure, and human resources, changes made to one will require adjustments in the others. For example, if the production line in a factory is replaced by a craft technology where teams work on whole projects together, the interactions among workers will be dramatically changed. If an employee enjoys interacting with a certain group of people, the new structure may lead to decreased motivation because of his or her having been removed from an enjoyable situation. Because of these interactions all three factors must be analyzed to see how each affects the other.

Technology is the easiest component to analyze and change. It is inanimate and has no attachment to old ways. The decision to change technology can be a financial or production decision. When new technology will contribute more to productivity than it will cost, then changes should be made. Changes in technology can have an extremely beneficial effect on productivity, but it is easy to forget that all of the factors of organizational performance are interrelated and changes in technology will require new skills from employees and new organizational structures. The effectiveness of the new technology will be constrained by the ability and willingness of the people involved to use it.

Changing the organizational structure is a complex process, because it directly affects people on the job. The structure itself has no attitudes or memory, but the people involved do. Changing the organization's structure changes responsibilities and relationships. New activities must be performed and new skills developed. While employees can handle these changes up to a certain point, too much disruption of their routines just cannot be absorbed. Changes in structure therefore have to be analyzed in terms of what new requirements and pressures will be put on the employees involved.

Changing human resources is the most complex of all organizational changes because people are unpredictable. They like old ways and have individual preferences. Changing skills and activities will be limited by the organization's structure and technology. Skills learned in a laboratory or classroom will be retained and used only if they match the technology and structure of the job. If new skills are never used, they will be forgotten.

It should be apparent from the foregoing discussion that no matter which job component is changed to change activities, all of the rest will be affected. Technology affects structure, structure affects human resources, and the human resources will determine the effectiveness technology and structure. Changes in job activities therefore require a thorough analysis of all of the components of organizational performance.

MONITORING PROGRESS

To evaluate changes after they are made, employee performance must be monitored. This critical step in job design is often forgotten. The interactions among technology, structure, and human resources are so complex that changes to them won't always have the anticipated effect. Further adjustments may be necessary. In fact, often the only way to determine how job changes will affect performance is to select a subsample of jobs, try some changes, and see what happens. If the changes work out well, they can be extended to the rest of the jobs. Once this is done, the jobs must be monitored to make sure everyone focuses on their performance objectives. It is so easy to become so involved in new ways, new relationships, and new skills etc., that you forget the purpose of the job is to achieve results. The results achieved should determine the value of any changes made. Monitoring results is done by using the techniques reviewed in Chapter Three.

SUMMARY

Activities are the behavioral manifestation of all the advance preparations of performance, goal setting, discussions, directing, training, etc. If employees fail because their activities are misdirected and inappropriate, all the preparation goes for naught. Managers manage job activities by:

1. analyzing the job.
2. changing the technology, structure, and/or human resources.
3. monitoring progress.

EIGHT CONTROLLING REWARDS

INTRODUCTION

Rewards are what employees receive for performing well. Sometimes these rewards come from the organization in the form of money, recognition, and promotions. Other times, rewards may consist of feelings from having performed well. Because rewards are such powerful motivators of performance, you should know what they are and how they are managed.

According to Skinner (Skinner, 1969), a reward is a reinforcer. A reinforcer is something the individual values and finds satisfying. Behaviors for which the person receives a reinforcer are likely to be repeated.

The assumptions for using rewards as a way of influencing people in organizations are: (1) people will engage in activities that are most likely to produce satisfying personal results; (2) when people receive what satisfies them as a result of certain behavior, they will be more likely to repeat those behaviors in the future; and (3) management has clearly defined good performance and can reward employees when they perform well.

With these assumptions in mind, we can manage rewards by (1) determining what rewards the employee finds satisfying and (2) making the rewards available when the person performs well.

WHAT IS REWARDING TO THE EMPLOYEE?

The key to rewarding performance is to remember the worker defines what is rewarding, not management. Management may be able to affect what people want by denying or bestowing rewards. You can underpay people and they will want money, or you can swamp people with so much responsibility they will be glad to be relieved of some of it rather than seeing it as a reward for having done well in the past. In the final analysis, however, management cannot coerce people into accepting and being excited about the rewards they wish to distribute. In order to reward properly, management must understand employees well enough to know what they find rewarding.

Rewards people enjoy can be grouped into three categories: (1) physical, (2) social, and (3) growth. These rewards match what Alderfer (1969) refers to as existence, relatedness, and growth needs. The advantage of this classification is that it identifies rewards managers control. Physical rewards relate to existence needs and refer to compensation, benefits, office space, cars, equipment, computers, etc. Anything tangible that can be given to employees is a physical reward. Social rewards relate to relatedness needs and come from other people in the form of acceptance into a group, recognition and praise, verbal reinforcement, etc.; these relate to the love and esteem needs that Maslow refers to. Growth rewards come from succeeding at tasks and developing personal skills and abilities.

Management controls rewards in each category. Compensation and benefits fill physical needs. Group identification, praise, and recognition fill social needs. Career development and skill improvement fill growth needs. Some rewards fill more than one category. Financial rewards, for example, can relate to all three areas. The tendency might be to automatically assume money is a physical reward and will relate to people's physical needs. But money relates to social and growth and accomplishment needs also. Money may not buy you friends but it does often determine where you live, what you do, who you associate with, how you dress, your outside activities, etc. Money serves as recognition for accomplishment and as feedback for past performance. Money should not be looked at only as a physical reward.

Because most people at one time or another want each of the three kinds of rewards, managers must make provisions for all of them. Organizational reward systems for all of them have to be in place so management can provide different reinforcements for good performance.

MAKING THE REWARDS AVAILABLE WHEN THE PERSON PERFORMS WELL

The relationship between performance and rewards is referred to as the contingency of reinforcement. The relationship is not automatic and must be established in each organization. The relationship between performance and reward can be designed numerous ways, each with its cost and benefits. Throughout the discussion that follows, remember rewards are oriented to any of the wants people have: physical, social, or growth.

Systems Rewards

Systems rewards are those given to people for being members of and participating in an organization, group, job, etc. Compensation and benefits are systems rewards when given solely on the basis of membership in an organization. Some monetary rewards are also systems rewards; life and medical insurance policies and other benefits that everyone in the organization receives. Across-the-board raises in which everyone receives a fixed amount as well as promotions and raises based on tenure in the organization are also systems rewards.

Social and growth rewards can also be made available as systems rewards. A supervisor's approval given to everyone who comes to work is a systems reward. The recognition and the opportunities to learn that a person receives for being a part of a particular group are also systems rewards.

Systems rewards are best for motivating participation because that is what they recognize. People stay in organizations because of what they receive for being a member. Systems rewards are important but have interesting consequences. Systems rewards often define the minimum level at which people will be satisfied. Increasing the systems rewards simply raises the minimum level expected before people become dissatisfied. Consider the following example.

A large lumber mill in the western United States had a good year. Profits were up and management wanted to say thank you to the employees. Management had meetings and decided to surprise the workers on Thanksgiving with a turkey to serve as a small token of appreciation. They developed elaborate plans for buying and delivering the turkeys so that no one would find out. They printed up cards of appreciation. As the workers left Wednesday for the Thanksgiving holidays, management stood at the gate handing out the turkeys. The workers were surprised. Management was pleased and everything seemed to work out well.

The next year a month before Thanksgiving, the personnel department started getting memos and letters asking where and when the turkeys would be distributed. Some of the employees thought it would be good to plan ahead this Thanksgiving. Management didn't have any excess profits that year and hadn't any plans to distribute turkeys. They told personnel to distribute an announcement thanking the employees for their continued effort in the past year and explaining that because of economic conditions, no turkeys would be distributed. The employees responded quite unfavorably to the announcement; even threatening a short-term walkout in protest. Relationships were strained to such a point that management finally relented and bought turkeys for everyone. The next year, prior to Thanksgiving, the personnel department again received memos and letters asking where to pick up the turkeys. This time a small group of employees indicated they didn't like turkey, they preferred a roast or ham and suggested management might want to consider a ham option. Management balked but finally relented once again. The following year, management could see what was coming and decided not to turn into a grocery store so they negotiated the cost of a 20-pound turkey as a Thanksgiving bonus into the contract.

When the employees complained, they received the turkeys they wanted; thus their behavior was reinforced. The attitude among the employees is a common response to systems rewards, "What I have, you owe me and in order to increase my satisfaction and commitment, you need to go higher." The obvious next question is how long will people be satisfied with the new level of reward? Typically the answer is, not long. Systems rewards are crucial for attracting and holding employees, but they entail attitudinal consequences that must be monitored carefully.

Individual Rewards

Individual rewards are given employees for accomplishing defined goals and responsibilities (e.g., selling the product, accomplishing the objective, completing the project). Individual rewards are based on the assumption that showing up is not enough, you must accomplish something. Individual rewards can be given two ways: continuous reinforcement where the reward is given each time the person performs properly, or intermittent rewards on some schedule where the rewards come only after multiple responses.

Continuous Rewards Continuous reinforcement—for example pay received after each sale—has limited usefulness in organizations: first because the desired behavior will increase very rapidly while rewarded but will rapidly worsen when the reward is removed, creating a see-saw effect. Second because monitoring and rewarding performance continuously is almost impossible. Managers cannot follow their employees around and reward them every time they do something right. Organizations have to develop intermittent reward schedules.

Intermittent Rewards Intermittent rewards can follow four different schedules. The amount of the reward is the same in each schedule but the timing differs as seen in the following list and Figure 8-1.

1. *Fixed Interval Schedule.* The person is rewarded after a certain period of time. An academic course including a fixed midterm and final has a fixed interval schedule. This schedule creates peaks and valleys of effort; all-night cram sessions just before the test are characteristic of fixed interval schedules.
2. *Variable Interval Schedule.* Rewards are given on an average of elapsed time, but the time interval between any two of the rewards will be random. This approach obviously will not work well for pay plans because employees want to know when they are being paid. It does work well for nonmonetary rewards, however. A supervisor who visits an office on the average of three times a day at different times each day to give praise and recognition is operating on a variable interval schedule.
3. *Fixed Ratio Schedule.* The employee is rewarded only after a certain level

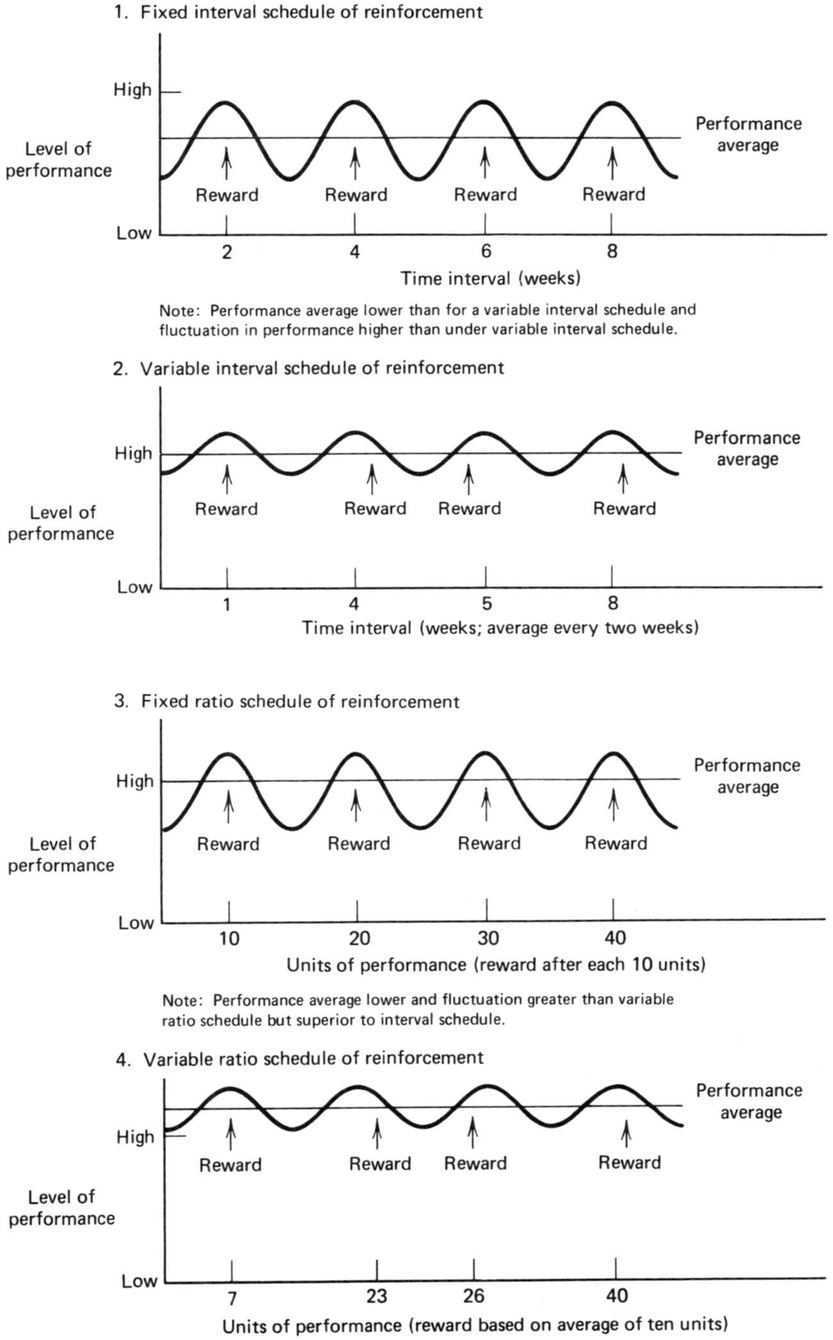

Figure 8-1 Intermittent rewards. (*Source:* W. C. Hamner and D. W. Organ, *Organizational Behavior; An Applied Psychological Approach,* Business Publications, Inc., Dallas, Texas, 1978, p. 55.)

of performance has been achieved. Piecework follows this schedule: after you make 50 units, you are paid so much per item. Like the fixed interval schedule, the fixed ratio schedule produces variability in performance, but the mean level of performance will be higher. Performance builds up until the point at which it is rewarded, then decreases.

4. *Variable Ratio Schedule.* The rewards are given only after a number of desired responses. On the average, the number of desired responses changes around the average. Thus a person working on a 15 to 1 variable ratio schedule might receive the rewards after 10 responses, then 20 responses, then 15 responses, and so on. Gambling is an example of a variable ratio schedule. The slot machine is set up to pay out a certain percentage of the money payed on a random schedule. Under this schedule, performance is usually maintained at a higher level because the person never knows when the reward is coming.

Some rewards, such as money, cannot be adapted to all of these schedules. Social and growth rewards are usually more flexible and can be adapted to variable schedules.

WHAT HAPPENS IF REWARDS AREN'T TIED TO GOOD PERFORMANCE

Rewards should be tied to good performance using either continuous or intermittent schedules; if they are not, they will motivate whatever behavior they recognize. Kerr (1978) has written an article entitled "The Folly of Hoping for A While Rewarding B" in which he presents several examples of what happens if you don't tie rewards to the type of behavior you want.

Politics

Official goals are "purposely vague and general and do not indicate . . . the host of decisions that must be made among alternative ways of achieving official goals and the priority of multiple goals . ." (1). They usually may be relied on to offend absolutely no one, and in this sense can be considered high-acceptance, low-quality goals. An example might be "build better schools." Operative goals are higher in quality but lower in acceptance, since they specify where the money will come from, what alternative goals will be ignored, etc.

The American citizenry supposedly wants its candidates for public office to set forth operative goals, making their proposed programs "perfectly clear," specifying sources and uses of funds, etc. However, since operative goals are lower in acceptance, and since aspirants to public office need acceptance (from at least 50.1 percent of the people), most politicians prefer to speak only of official goals, at least until after the election. They, of course, would agree to speak at the operative level if "punished" for not doing so. The electorate could do this by refusing to support candidates who do not speak at the operative level.

Instead, however, the American voter typically punishes (witholds support from) candidates who frankly discuss where the money will come from, rewards politicians who speak only of official goals, but hopes that candidates (despite the reward system) will discuss the issues operatively. It is academic whether it was moral for Nixon, for example, to refuse to discuss his 1968 "secret plan" to end the Vietnam war, his 1972 operative goals concerning the lifting of price controls, the reshuffling of his cabinet, etc. The point is that the reward system made such refusal rational.

It seems worth mentioning that no manuscript can adequately define what is "moral" and what is not. However, examination of costs and benefits, combined with knowledge of what motivates a particular individual, often will suffice to determine what for him is "rational." If the reward system is so designed that it is irrational to be moral, this does not necessarily mean that immorality will result. But is this not asking for trouble?

War

If some oversimplification may be permitted, let it be assumed that the primary goal of the organization (Pentagon, Luftwaffe, or whatever) is to win. Let it be assumed further that the primary goal of most individuals on the front lines is to get home alive. Then there appears to be an important conflict in goals—personally rational behavior by those at the bottom will endanger goal attainment by those at the top.

But not necessarily! It depends on how the reward system is set up. The Vietnam war was indeed a study of disobedience and rebellion, with terms such as "fragging" (killing one's own commanding officer) and "search and evade" becoming part of the military vocabulary. The difference in subordinates' acceptance of authority between World War II and Vietnam is reported to be considerable, and veterans of the Second World War often have been quoted as being outraged at the mutinous actions of many American soldiers in Vietnam.

Consider, however, some critical differences in the reward system in use during the two conflicts. What did the GI in World War II want? To go home. And when did he get to go home? When the war was won! If he disobeyed the orders to clean out the trenches and take the hills, the war would not be won and he would not go home. Furthermore, what were his chances of attaining his goal (getting home alive) if he obeyed the orders compared to his chances if he did not? What is being suggested is that the rational soldier in World War II, *whether patriotic or not,* probably found it expedient to obey.

Consider the reward system in use in Vietnam. What did the man at the bottom want? To go home. And when did he get to go home? When his tour of duty was over! This was the case *whether or not* the war was won. Furthermore, concerning the relative chance of getting home alive by disobeying orders compared to the chance if they were disobeyed, it is worth noting that a mutineer in Vietnam was far more likely to be assigned rest and rehabilitation (on the assumption that fatigue was the cause) than he was to suffer any negative consequence.

In his description of the "zone of indifference," Barnard stated that "a person can and will accept a communication as authoritative only when . . . at the time of his decision, he believes it to be compatible with his personal interests as a whole" (2). In light of the reward system used in Vietnam, would it not have been personally irrational for some orders to have been obeyed? Was not the military implementing a system which *rewarded* disobedience, while *hoping* that soldiers (despite the reward system) would obey orders?

Medicine

Theoretically, a physician can make either of two types of error, and intuitively one seems as bad as the other. A doctor can pronounce a patient sick when he is actually well, thus causing his needless anxiety and expense, curtailment of enjoyable foods and activities, and even physical danger by subjecting him to needless medication and surgery. Alternatively, a doctor can label a sick person well, and thus avoid treating what may be a serious, even fatal ailment. It might be natural to conclude that physicians seek to minimize both types of error.

Such a conclusion would be wrong. It is estimated that numerous Americans are presently afflicted with iatrogenic (physician *caused*) illnesses (3). This occurs when the doctor is approached by someone complaining of a few stray symptoms. The doctor classifies and organizes the symptoms, gives them a name, and obligingly tells the patient what further symptoms may be expected. This information often acts as a self-fulfilling prophecy, with the result that, from that day on, the patient for all practical purposes is sick.

Why does this happen? Why are physicians so reluctant to sustain a type 2 error (pronouncing a sick person well) that they will tolerate many type 1 errors? Again, a look at the reward system is needed. The punishments for a type 2 error are real: guilt, embarrassment, and the threat of lawsuit and scandal. On the other hand, a type 1 error (labeling a well person sick) "is sometimes seen as sound clinical practice, indicating a healthy, conservative approach to medicine" (3). Type 1 errors also are likely to generate increased income and a stream of steady customers who, being well in a limited physiological sense, will not embarrass the doctor by dying abruptly.

Fellow physicians and the general public therefore are really *rewarding* type 1 errors and at the same time *hoping* fervently that doctors will try not to make them.

References

1. Perrow, Charles, "The Analysis of Goals in Complex Organizations," in A. Etzioni (Ed.), *Readings on Modern Organizations* (Englewood Cliffs, N.J.: Prentice-Hall, 1969).
2. Barnard, Chester I. *The Functions of the Executive* (Cambridge, Mass.: Harvard University Press, 1964).
3. Scheff, Thomas J. "Decision Rules, Types of Error, and Their Consequences in Medical Diagnosis," in F. Massarik and P. Ratoosh (Eds.), *Mathematical Explorations in Behavioral Science* (Homewood, Ill.: Irwin 1965).

WHICH SHOULD WE USE: SYSTEMS VERSUS INDIVIDUAL REWARDS?[1]

We have talked about two ways of distributing rewards, one based on membership (systems rewards) and one based on performing the job as

[1]The following discussion adapted from L. S. Baird, "Managing Dissatisfaction," *Personnel,* May–June, pp. 12–21, © 1981 AMACOM, a division of American Management Associations, New York. All rights reserved.

defined (individual rewards). Comparing two hypothetical companies, one using systems rewards and the other individual rewards, dramatic differences exist between them in the long run. Consider the following hypothetical example:

In Company A, people are rewarded according to their job performance; high performers (50 percent) get 10 percent raises each year, low performers (50 percent) receive no raises. Nearby, a similar organization (Company B) distributes rewards on the basis of membership; everyone receives 5 percent raises each year. Figure 8-2 shows what happens over the years. Over the short term, the two companies are similar, but over a period of time the differences add up. After 10 years high performers are making $10,000 more than low performers in the organization rewarding job performance. In the organization giving systems rewards, everyone is making the same.

Consider the movement of human resources likely to take place over 10 years. The low performers in Company A receiving the individual rewards (no raises, $15,000) want more rewards. One way to obtain them is by staying in Company A and increasing their performance. The problem is that the best they can hope for is a 10 percent raise. Moving to Company B, when low performers are making $23,269 is preferable. If performance is rewarded according to membership in the other organization low performers can move over at a much higher salary based on a claim of experience. Even if that is not possible, raises in the future will be automatic and the person can continue to do what he or she has been doing, performing poorly and still receive raises. Thus, systems rewards will attract the low performers from other organizations. Not only will new low performers be attracted but the low performers already there will have an incentive to remain. They are making more money now than they could make in other organizations that reward according to performance.

	Individual Rewards		Systems Rewards	
	Low Performers —0—	High Performers 10 percent	Low Performers 5 percent	High Performers 5 percent
1st year	$15,000	$15,000	$15,000	$15,000
2nd year	15,000	16,500	15,750	15,750
3rd year	15,000	18,150	16,537	16,537
4th year	15,000	19,965	17,364	17,364
5th year	15,000	21,961	18,232	18,232
10th year	15,000	35,368	23,269	23,269

Figure 8-2 Salaries of high and low performers.

Now consider what is happening in the organization where job performance is rewarded. The high performers are probably going to stay and continue to perform well. The high performers from Company B will also be attracted because they can increase their pay ($23,269 to $35,368). Company B, which pays for performance, could offer high performers from other organization an immediate $5000 raise plus the potential of further rewards according to performance in the future. They are willing to pay high performers more because high performers produce so much more.

Of course we have made severely simplifying assumptions, but, all things being equal, when individual and systems rewards exist together, systems rewards drive out high performers and lock in low performers while individual rewards drive out low performers and attract high performers. Systems rewards reward membership and that is the type of results they create. Individual rewards reward performance on the job and that is the type of results they create. Systems rewards cannot be used to create job performance. If organizations are interested in job performance they must be willing to reward it. If they are interested in people joining and staying in the organization they must be willing to reward that. In most cases you will be interested in both and will have to have both individual and systems rewards.

We have used money to illustrate the differences between individual and systems rewards. The concepts apply to all the other types of rewards a manager controls, of course. Praise, recognition, and growth opportunities can all be given for membership or job performance and must be managed correctly.

SHOULD WE BE CONCERNED ABOUT THE ATTITUDES OF PEOPLE?

Considerable time and energy is spent in organizations assessing attitudes and keeping people happy. If the purpose of organization is performance, should we really be concerned about the attitudes of our employees? For a lot of reasons the answer is yes, we should, but we should consider satisfaction from a management point of view, that is, one that is concerned with performance. We have discussed two competing approaches to human behavior: cognitive and behavioral; both support management's concern with attitudes. Cognitive theorists suggest that a manager should be concerned about employee satisfaction because it will affect future performance. They state that people are likely to do those things that they expect will fill their unmet needs. Knowing how satisfied a person is makes it possible to predict what needs he or she will try to fill in the future.

Behavioral theorists define attitudes as "an individual's predisposition to evaluate a stimulus in a favorable or an unfavorable manner. . ." (i.e., "a person's readiness to respond to that stimulus object"). Behavioral theorists believe that management should be concerned about attitudes because they are indications of a person's readiness to respond. Attitudes help to predict how a person will react.

Even though employee satisfaction is important, it should not be the sole basis of management decisions. We need to know not only who is satisfied or dissatisfied but why. Consider the following cases.

Greg is on the sales force of a hospital supply corporation. He receives a base salary of $6000 plus commissions. Commissions are based on dollar sales and are such that the total annual salary for salespersons ranges from $10,000 to $50,000. Greg is a low performer presently making $12,000 ($6000 base plus commission). He is barely surviving and very dissatisfied.

Colleen is a high performer in the administrative offices of a large corporation. She completes each assignment extremely well. Colleen complains that she is never recognized for her fine work. She receives the same salary as everyone else and says her chances for promotion don't seem promising.

George is performing poorly in his job as supervisor of a small engineering shop. He knows his performance is low, and so does everyone else. His attitude is: "So what, as long as you don't blow it too bad, you'll make the same money as everyone else. All you have to do is stay around here long enough."

In Greg's case, the management problem is how to motivate the employee, give him the skills to perform better, and thus improve his earnings. In Colleen's case, the problem is to prevent a high performer from translating her dissatisfaction into reduced performance or, worse yet, leaving the organization. In George's case, it's the manager who is likely to be dissatisfied. George is relatively happy; he is getting what he wants and unless something is changed, will probably continue to do what he has done in the past—perform poorly.

As the foregoing cases show, employee satisfaction or dissatisfaction is not a sufficient basis for management action; further information is needed. If the low performers are dissatisfied, management must spend the time and money to help them become high performers so they can gain satisfaction from their work. If the high performers are dissatisfied, the management systems in use are creating problems. High performers should be rewarded and encouraged. If they are dissatisfied, their performance is likely to worsen or they may leave the organization altogether.

Thus, from both a cognitive and behavioral viewpoint, knowing who is satisfied or dissatisfied and for what reason is important. An attitude survey can identify who is satisfied or dissatisfied in the organization, then management must find out what type of performers they are and what other options they have. Consider for example, what satisfaction and dissatisfaction mean in the following situations.

Low Peformance—Average Rewards—Nowhere to Go

This is a potential situation when everyone is given the same reward regardless of their performance. Examples are insurance policies and health plans when everyone receives the same amount, pay when distributed as a fixed sum, or praise that is general and given to everyone, etc.

In these situations many attractive options are not open to employees. Because they are low performers they are already over rewarded. Unless they change, other organizations are not likely to offer them more. They aren't likely to search for other options, either. They are relatively satisfied because of the rewards they are receiving. These employees probably will stay and continue to do what they have been doing in the past—perform poorly.

Low Performance—Low Rewards—Nowhere to Go

This situation potentially exists in organizations that vary rewards according to performance. Low performance results in low rewards. The employees will be dissatisfied and interested in changing the situation. They probably won't have any attractive options in other organizations because no one wants low performers. This leaves the other alternatives: increased effort, sabotage, or apathy.

Employees will choose increased effort if they think it will lead to what they want. Two conditions must exist before employees are likely to hold this belief. First, employees must believe they have the ability to perform. People won't try things they know they can't do. Second, they must believe their performance will be rewarded.

If these two conditions don't exist, frustration results. Which of the two remaining options people choose in response to their frustration will be determined by how important the desired results were initially. The more important the hoped-for result, the more violent will be the reaction when it is not obtained. If it was quite important, the response is likely to be sabotage. If it wasn't too critical the individual will probably just withdraw and do the minimum necessary to remain in the organization.

High Performers—Low-to-Average Rewards—Other Options

This situation usually exists when everyone is paid the same or if the rewards are given based on something other than performance, (i.e., friendship, social status, or tenure). If performance is not recognized, the high performers have no reason to stay. If other places are willing to pay the premium that goes with outstanding performance, people will leave.

High Performers—Low-to-Average Rewards—Nowhere to Go

Sometimes high performers do not have any options. The labor market is such that mobility isn't possible. This could be the most explosive of all situations. The high performers have the potential for the highest payoff, which means if they are not recognized they also suffer the biggest loss. Under normal circumstances they would leave. However, with all other options blocked, sabotage or apathy are the available alternatives.

IMPLICATIONS FOR MANAGEMENT

The challenge, of course, is to create situations such that both satisfied and dissatisfied employees choose to perform and increase their efforts. Attitudes are not the main concern of management but they are important warning flags. If we know the nature of the reward systems and what options are available, employees' attitudes will help us understand what employees might be doing in the future. The situations described above can be used to suggest some general guidelines for managing attitudes so they can be translated into a positive force for organizational performance.

Reward Performance

If performance isn't being rewarded, something else is, for example, group membership, who you know, tenure, luck, etc. The people receiving the rewards will be satisfied but the high performers won't. Thus, the high performers are the ones most likely to be dissatisfied and engage in counterproductive behavior. Because their expectations are high, their loss and negative responses are likely to be great. What worsens the situation is that the high performers are the ones with the skills and energy to really destroy the organization if they want to.

Several conditions are necessary to reward performance. First, good performance has to be defined. Without a definition of good performance, you can not determine how people's dissatisfaction relates to performance. You have no way to give individuals a goal or determine whether they have succeeded. Second, the benefits and opportunities available for performance have to be seen as rewards. Remember the employee defines what is rewarding, not the manager. In some cases performance itself might be rewarding. In others it might be the money or the praise and recognition associated with the money. The manager has to find out what is rewarding to the individual.

Don't Rely Solely on the Attitude Survey

Attitude surveys have been a staple in the manager's kit bag for quite some time. Surveys provide valuable information if used properly. They can also yield disastrous results. For example, assume an attitude survey indicates satisfaction is low. You also know productivity could be improved. You have heard about rewarding performance and decide a merit system should be implemented. After a few months, to the surprise of everyone, things do not improve, they worsen. The attitude surveys show satisfaction has gone down. After a few more months you finally give up and go back to the old system.

The attitude survey seems to indicate that implementing the merit system was a bad idea. However, consider what might have been happening. This time ask two questions: Who is dissatisfied and why? The low performers, who were receiving an average level of pay, are dissatisfied because they now receive less under the merit plan. If the unit has more low performers than high performers, the average level of satisfaction will decline.

Asking the second question "Why are they dissatisfied?" sheds new light on the problem. Now instead of concluding that the management systems need to be changed, the manager should be able to say to the employee: "I understand you are dissatisfied. We both know how you can be more satisfied. Perform better so that you can obtain the rewards available for good performance. Let's work on improving your performance."

Research suggests that having overall satisfaction decline when people are rewarded according to their performance may not be uncommon. In one study (Baird and Hamner, 1979), individuals worked under two different incentive systems. Those who were paid according to their performance were substantially less satisfied, on the average, than those who were given a flat rate. Even more interesting is a study by Greene and Podsakoff (1978). They investigated what happened to attitudes and performance when a merit system was replaced by a flat rate system. They found that satisfaction with pay went up and performance went down (Figure 8-3). Further analysis indicated that under the flat rate system, a sizable group of low performers were now making more money than when pay was given according to performance. They were more satisfied, and the average level of satisfaction went up. Remember, however, that productivity went down.

The average level of satisfaction may indeed initially go down when people are rewarded according to their performance. If the only question asked is "what is the level of satisfaction?" some erroneous conclusions may

Dependent Variable	Before Change (merit system) Mean	Before Change (merit system) Standard Deviation	After Change (flat rate) Mean	After Change (flat rate) Standard Deviation	Change Before/After
Satisfaction with work	35.61	13.44	33.27	10.77	−2.34
Pay	16.09	13.95	18.39	16.33	+2.30
Promotion	16.72	12.67	15.91	13.57	− .81
Supervision	35.44	9.56	37.01	11.22	+1.57
Co-workers	39.47	11.33	40.67	10.44	+1.20
Performance	5.40	2.91	4.89	2.10	− .51

Figure 8-3 Change in satisfaction and performance when merit system was replaced by flat rate.

be drawn and faulty management practices implemented to raise satisfaction. Find out who is dissatisfied and why. Then management is better equiped to translate dissatisfaction into increased productivity.

Assist Individuals to Translate Satisfaction and Dissatisfaction into Positive Actions

A natural tendency exists to try and keep people happy. The reasons are often not particularly humanitarian, we just do not want to deal with the problems of dissatisfied people. When employees don't get what they want, they immediately want to know why. They become defensive and hostile. They want reasons and justification. If they don't receive them in understandable form, they are likely to withdraw, leave, or sabotage the organization. It is far easier to avoid the whole issue by rating and rewarding everyone a little above average. Of course that really doesn't solve problems, it just creates a different group of dissatisfied employees, the high performers. The issue then is not how to stop making people dissatisfied. The issue is making sure the right people are dissatisfied and then developing the support systems necessary to help them translate their dissatisfaction into positive action.

If the high performers are dissatisfied, it is probably because the rewards aren't related to performance. The best thing to do is to move the rewards back in line with performance. If that can't be done with the monetary rewards it should at least be possible with praise, recognition, job assignments, and other rewards for doing good work. If it can't be done with any of the rewards, brace yourself and hope the high performers give some advance warning before they leave or start destroying the organization.

If the reward systems are designed properly, the high performers will be satisfied and the low performers will be dissatisfied because they aren't receiving the rewards they want. The question is how to keep the high performers motivated and help low performers turn their dissatisfaction into increased effort, skills, and performance.

The best way to understand the type of support system necessary to translate attitudes into performance is to consider what responses the organization is trying to encourage and what it wants to prevent. Employees leave if they are not receiving what they want and see no possibility of obtaining it in their present position. They withdraw or engage in sabotage if no other options are available. The objective is to develop support systems that make it possible for those who have ability and motivation to stay and try to do better. Those who have neither ability nor motivation should be assisted in relocating. The following list gives some suggestions that would make this possible.

1. *Clearly Define Responsibilities and Desired Results.* When a dissatisfied employee comes marching into the supervisor's office to find out why he or she wasn't promoted, or why the job isn't structured differently, or why a new assignment was given, supervisors need to be able to provide answer. They need to be able to explain what was expected and how the employee's performance compared to the desired result. If performance can't be clearly defined, management shouldn't pretend that it can. They should say that it can't and be willing to explain the other bases for their decisions.
2. *Understand and Be Able to Describe What Contributes to Performance.* Performance is the end product. It is what happens as a result of the employee's effort and abilities. Just telling someone they have performed poorly isn't enough. Management's job is to understand why performance is poor and what can be done to improve. This will require an understanding of what skills, behaviors, processes, etc. lead to good performance. Then the response to the question, "Why aren't I being rewarded?" can be, "Because you haven't performed well. Here's why, and here's what you and I need to do in the future to improve your performance."
3. *Development and Training.* If performance is low because the employee lacks skills, pressure for performance can only lead to frustration. Usually the harder we try when we don't know how to do something, the worse we do. We need to step back and spend some time and energy developing the appropriate skills. Once the skills are learned, pressure for production will have positive results.

   During the learning period particularly, managers need to do more than just tell someone they have performed poorly. The employee needs to know what he or she is doing wrong and how to improve. The main focus of the manager and the worker's attention shouldn't be on the final results. It should be on how to achieve them.

4. *Understand the Environment Within Which the Employee Is Working.* In certain situations employees do not control what he or she is able to accomplish. They fail with no apparent reason for failure. One of the manager's first jobs is to help the individual analyze the situation and discover the causes of failure. Together they can then attack the problems.

   When an individual has failed and the reasons are beyond his or her control, the supervisor needs to be as supportive as possible. Unforseen circumstances sometimes get in the way. The best that can be done is to say you understand and wish them better luck next time.

5. *Develop Active Career Counseling and Placement Programs.* Jobs and people change. What was once rewarding can become routine and dissatisfying. This change can happen for any number of reasons. The job may change so that it no longer matches the skills and interests of the individual. The individual may change so that what was once challenging is now repetitive and monotonous. The individual may even have been misplaced on the job in the first place. He or she is able to perform the job well but finds it unrewarding.

   In some cases, adjusting the job or the individual to obtain a better match is futile. The manager should instead help the individual reassess him or herself and find a new position.

   Counseling and placement can become preventive as well as corrective programs. For example, a consulting firm recently implemented career counseling and placement as part of their recruiting program. The type of individuals they wanted were bright, aggressive, and management oriented. They were the type of people who had other options and didn't necessarily want to lock themselves into a consulting career. The firm developed a unique recruiting strategy. They let it be known that client firms were welcome to recruit staff from the consulting firm. Companies had an opportunity to observe and assess the competence of consultants working on their projects before they made job offers. A consulting job could be viewed as a "tryout" with neither side making a firm commitment until after they saw how it was working out.

   Employees of the consulting organizations could "try out" many different organizations before deciding where to go. The consulting firm said to its employees, "Come work with us for three to five years. After that period, if you are enjoying the work and are productive, we can promote you up the management ladder in the consulting firm. Many of our employees find, however, that after a while they really want to try their hand at managing rather than telling others how to do it. We have an active career counseling program to help you choose the proper organization to join next. We can even pick some assignments to make sure you get exposure to the types of organizations you are interested in." Basically they were saying, "We expect you to be a high performer while you are here, but when your interests change, we can help you get where you want to go."

Most organizations can take the same approach. A mismatch between the individual and the job is just as much the responsibility of the organization as it is the employee's. People often outgrow their jobs. Turnover can be a positive factor if managed correctly. It provides expanded opportunities and challenges for those whose capabilities have exceeded the job. It brings in fresh energy and ideas, and it transfers people whose capabilities can never become equal to the job. In order to manage turnover correctly, however, career counseling and placement programs have to become part of the normal operating procedures of the organization.

SUMMARY

Rewards are the outcomes employees receive for performing. If managers can provide rewards when employees do well, they will motivate performance. Attitudes are important because they provide an indication of what the person will do in the future.

NINE
MANAGING FEEDBACK

INTRODUCTION

Evaluating performance and then giving feedback is the component of management that makes performance improvement and learning possible. Using feedback, actual results can be compared with goals as the basis for whatever adjustments need to be made. Problems and errors can be identified and corrected, goals can be clarified, and future operations streamlined. Without feedback, management is an endless process of setting goals and then wondering what has happened; decisions are made based on guesses and premonitions. Unfortunately, that may sound all too familiar to some managers who spend hours filling in forms, explaining their goals, and then filing the forms in their bottom drawers where they will not be seen or used until time to set next year's goals.

Because feedback is so critical for effective management, it is important to understand what kinds of information can be useful in the feedback process. In this chapter we consider (1) the types of information collected and reported, (2) formats for feeding information back to employees, (3) characteristics of useful information, (4) the nature of the feedback system (i.e., who gets the information and how should it be provided?).

TYPES OF INFORMATION COLLECTED AND REPORTED

Facts and figures, numbers, impressions, and feelings are all information and can be used to describe past experience. In and of itself, this information is useless; it only becomes useful when communicated. We define this communicating of information about past performance as feedback.

Various kinds of information are available throughout the performance process. Information about the desired results identifies the target. Process-related information deals with the activities and processes necessary to accomplish the work (e.g., descriptions of interpersonal interactions, reporting relationships, and communication). Outcome-related information deals with what has been accomplished (e.g., the number and quality of units produced). Information about all the stages of performance is available and should be used. Understanding what is happening at one point in the performance process is not enough.

For example, in one study by Frohman (1977) the researchers were interested in why employees were performing poorly. They hypothesized three reasons: (1) there was not enough effort, (2) there was misunderstanding of how to do the job, and (3) there was lack of goal clarity. The researchers found that only 30 percent of the mistakes made by workers could be attributed to lack of effort. Forty percent were caused by misunderstanding the activities required and another 30 percent were the result of unclear goals. Taken together, most of the problems were caused by the employees' misunderstanding of what the organization expected them to do. This problem could have been solved with proper feedback about activities and expected results.

Consider the following example of the importance of both process (what is being done) and outcome (what is accomplished) information being fed back. A state agency was involved in safety inspections; they inspected all types of equipment ranging from boilers and fire extinguishers to ski lifts and carnival rides. Goals were set for the number of inspections to be carried out monthly. Information on accomplishments was collected by way of daily reports on the number and type of inspections completed. This information was sent in and filed but was not tabulated until the year-end reports were due. Top management heard about the importance of employee involvement in decision making and decided to redesign the job to give the employees more freedom and more involvement in the planning of their work activities, but they didn't change the nature of the information the employee would receive about their performance. Management continued to establish goals and employees continued to send in their reports. But the employees still received no information about how well they were doing. The organization in effect said, "Here's what you are supposed to accomplish. Now, go do what you want and, by the way, we are never going to let you know how you are doing."

Productivity as defined by the organization (number of inspections conducted, number of violations cited, number of training sessions conducted) went down considerably. When they investigated the problem, management found two different reactions to the new job designs. One group, which in the past tended to be the low producers, interpreted the changes as a license to retire. To them, the expanded responsibility meant they could do whatever they wanted and nobody was checking up on them. Unfortunately, this group of employees used their increased autonomy to reduce the time and effort they spent on the job; they began to plan their schedules to fit golf matches and lunches.

A second group (fortunately this included most of the employees) did in fact increase the time and effort they devoted to their jobs. They became much more involved in their work. These employees were highly skilled employees who had spent many years learning about different types of equipment and machinery. They not only made inspections, they usually made excellent suggestions about how to correct problems. Among these workers the number of inspections went down too, because they were spending much more time on each one. At the same time, the number of violations cited went down because instead of citing the organization when they found problems, the inspectors would show people how to fix them. The number of formal training sessions also went down because training began to be conducted on an informal basis. On every measure of productivity the organization used, these employees were less productive, but they never received any information to suggest that they weren't doing exactly what was expected.

Were the measures wrong or were the employees wrong? The agency has to decide. The inspectors were more effective in the organizations they serviced, but many organizations were not visited, and these gradually experienced a rise in accidents and injuries. If you worked in an organization where an accident was prevented because the inspectors were spending more time solving problems, you would think they were doing a good job. If you worked in an organization where a major accident happened because the inspectors never showed up, you would feel they were doing a bad job.

The point is that instead of making assumptions about each other, the inspectors and their managers should have agreed on productive use of time and developed information to monitor both the activities of the inspectors and the results of their work. The inspectors worked hard, and they assumed performance was good. The managers were becoming more and more frustrated and began firing employees, reducing pay, and transferring inspectors into desk jobs. Unfortunately, the only time the two sides ever talked about performance was when the management took these drastic actions. Not understanding their differences, the two sides became hostile towards each other rather than resolving the problems caused by lack of feedback.

In summary then, information is available about what has happened at each stage of the performance process. The key is to understand how to feed back information so that it will be most helpful to both employees and supervisors in managing performance. Ultimately, the manager controls the work environment, task assignment, and consequences of performance. The power to increase productivity and attain goals rests largely in the potential to effectively manage feedback.

FORMAT FOR FEEDING BACK INFORMATION

Once having decided what information is needed, the next step is choosing a format for relaying it to performers. The way in which performance information is communicated will often have as much or more influence on employee performance as the type of information given. Therefore, managers will have to define the appropriate method for each situation, and be able to implement it effectively.

The nature and use of information for feedback should be determined by the type of response needed to perform well on the job. Four types of responses can be elicited by different kinds of feedback: individualistic, competitive, cooperative, and helping.

Individualistic Behavior. Individualistic behavior focuses on maximizing one's own rewards (i.e., doing the best one can for oneself). This type of behavior is stimulated by giving the employee's information about his or her own performance as compared to a personal goal or the employee's own past performance. An example is, John sold $110.00 worth of product this month, a 20 percent increase over what he sold last month.

Competitive Behavior. Competitive behavior attempts to maximize a person's own rewards relative to those of another. The purpose is to beat the other person. This type of behavior is elicited by comparing one person's performance with another's. For example, John sold 20 percent more product than Sue.

Cooperative Behavior. The purpose of cooperative behavior is to maximize the rewards a group receives. This type of behavior happens most often when the information received combines one person's results with that of others. For example, District A, where John and Sue work, sold $230,000 worth of product last month.

Helping Behavior. Altruistic behavior attempts to maximize another person's reward. One person helps another succeed. This type of behavior is most often stimulated when one person has responsibility for another, and the information provided focuses on how the other person is performing. For example, Sue helped John sell $130,000 worth of product this month.

So we can refer to four types of feedback that match these types of behavior: individualistic, competitive, cooperative, and helping. Various combinations of these types of feedback are also possible. Feedback that compares one group's performance against another will result in cooperation within the group and competition among groups. Which of these formats is chosen will depend on the nature of the work situation and the type of behavior needed.

In *individualistic situations,* people work alone and are responsible for a major portion of the final product. They need data that give them information about their performance and focus their energies on performing well as an individual. This category would include authors, independent consultants, salespeople, and any type of job where the individual is responsible for all the stages of the performance process.

When people interact with others on the job and when accomplishment will be determined by the nature of these interactions, people need information about how others are doing. The way this information is given should be determined by whether it is a competitive, cooperative, or altruistic situation.

In *competitive situations* resources are limited. Whatever one person gets is not available for others. These are win/lose situations. Goals in competitive situations are stated in terms that compare one individual's performance against another's. How well an individual does will be determined by how poorly others do. Examples of competitive situations might occur in organizations that have limited budgets to divide among several departments or where there is a fixed amount of money available for salaries. In each of these cases comparative performance information should be given.

In *cooperative situations,* it is the results of all participants' effort that is important, that is, what the entire group is able to accomplish. A task force is a good example: it's not how each individual does, but how individuals perform as a group that counts. Sometimes this is a hard lesson for high-performing specialists to learn. Recently, a highly trained research scientist almost destroyed a small electronics firm by paying more attention to his own success as a scientist than to the commercial success of the firm's products. Many a group with individual "superstars" has failed because the stars were more concerned about their own performance than the performance of the group.

In an *helping situation,* the focus is on other people. Any type of helping situation has this characteristic. The objective is to improve someone else's performance. Most supervisor's jobs fall into this category. The supervisor is responsible for developing and managing his or her subordinates and is judged in terms of the subordinates' performance. In this case, as in all other helping tasks, the appropriate feedback is information about the performance of the person to be helped. (The discussion so far is summarized in Figure 9-1.)

Feedback should match the nature of the situation and the responses sought from the employees. If employees receive feedback on the number of loans that have been made, they will direct their energies toward making more loans. If they receive feedback on percentage defective products, they will focus their attention on reducing defects. If employees are informed about how well they are developing their staff, that is where their time and energy will be spent. If the feedback doesn't match the situation, the behavior won't either.

Nature of Situation	Appropriate Behavior	Appropriate Type of Feedback
Individualistic	Maximization of one's own gain—behavior is directed toward accomplishing individual goals.	Information concerning own prior and present performance.
Competitive	Relative gain maximization—the person attempts to outperform others with whom he or she is being compared.	Information concerning one's own and other people's prior performance.
Cooperative	Maximization of joint results—the person is concerned with the accomplishments of a group.	Information concerning the group's present and prior performance.
Helping	Maximization of another person's achievements—the individual's concern is improving the results achieved by others.	Information concerning another person's present and prior performance.

Figure 9-1 The nature and use of feedback.

Feedback in each of these situations will have a definite effect on what people do. An old management adage says, "Whatever is measured and reported will improve." Research hasn't specifically supported this contention yet, but its findings do, however, suggest that people will be much more aware of things that are measured and will direct their efforts toward them. Nadler (1977) lists three reasons employees are aware of and focus energy on what is measured.

1. *Implied Sanctions/Rewards.* Those being measured assume that if the managers are collecting data about a particular operation or program, it must be important. By implication, improved performance of important tasks will be rewarded. Employees are motivated to perform well.
2. *Evaluation.* Measurement increases the visibility of certain behaviors being evaluated, thereby facilitating comparisons. Activity will be generated in measured areas because, by implication, they are important and therefore rewardable.
3. *Explicit Rewards.* Data collection may be open and explicitly tied to desired outcomes. Behavior will be stimulated by availability of rewards.

In summary then, management must decide not only what information is appropriate but how it should be used to compare and evaluate performance. The nature and use of information given to employees must match the performance requirements of the situation. Management's first responsibility is to decide on what stage of the performance process to focus. This will identify the type of information that should be used. Then they have to decide what types of relationships they want to foster among the individuals in the organization. For certain tasks, a competitive relationship is necessary; for others, performance will not be very high unless cooperative or helping relationships are established. Once the nature of the desired relationships among employees is defined, the format for feeding information will be identified.

THE CHARACTERISTICS OF USEFUL INFORMATION

So far we have discussed the different types of performance information, and how it should be used as feedback. After understanding these concepts, the manager is ready to implement a system in which performance information can be fed back and used by employees. The best way to look at feedback on the individual level is as part of the helping process; feedback is given to help a person analyze his or her present status and make whatever changes are necessary to improve performance. Feedback tells a person how they are doing and what lies ahead (Gibb, 1961). Viewed in this way, performance information must have certain characteristics to be useful. These characteristics are important regardless of the focus of the feedback or the type of response desired.

Feedback Should Be Descriptive and Comprehensive

By describing situations as explicitly as possible, we are providing the information necessary for changes to take place. Descriptions make it possible for employees to compare the information they receive with their own perceptions. If the feedback covers all the major areas relevant to the situation, not just one area such as output, activities or inputs, it will be most useful.

Feedback Is Specific Rather Than General

Sometimes feedback in general terms is helpful (e.g., "You have done good work for us"). But it does far more good to be specific about what has been done (e.g., "The Turner project was excellent; it came in 10 percent under budget, was completed on time, and exceeded the original specifications").

Learning theory (Skinner, 1969) supports the idea that feedback should be specific. Thorndike's Law of Effect states that behavior positively reinforced will tend to be repeated; behavior leading to neutral or negative consequences tends not to be repeated. If employees have no knowledge of what behavior will be rewarded, they have no way to improve. Without specific information it becomes impossible to direct one's effort or learn from mistakes.

Feedback Should Be Directed Towards Factors That the Receiver Can Do Something About

Feedback should be directed towards activities and resources that employees can control. From social psychology we know that frustration is the result of blocked goal-oriented behavior. Providing employees with information about factors in the performance process over which they have no control, or for which they are not responsible, can only lead to frustration and withdrawal.

The Feedback Should Take into Account the Needs of Both the Giver and the Receiver

The manager needs predictable and continued productivity. Subordinates need information that not only lets them know how they have done, but increases their ability and motivation to perform well in the future. Both of these needs can be met if the manager recognizes the directing/learning function of feedback as well as its rewarding/motivating characteristics. Managers often use the information to evaluate and criticize, rather than as a tool for identifying and solving problems. If the manager focuses too heavily on the rewarding characteristics of feedback, employees will be motivated but have no guidance or direction for future activity. It is much like blowing up a balloon as tight as possible and then releasing it. Without some type of guidance system the balloon darts about randomly.

The Feedback is Appropriately Timed

In general, the sooner feedback is received after the activity has been performed, the better. The longer the time between the two, the less likely you are to remember what was done so that it can be repeated or changed. Time also reduces the chance of directly relating the reward to the results. The only case where this has not been found to be true is in complex learning or problem-solving situations. In these cases the individuals need feedback, but they also need time to reflect on what they have learned and to engage in problem-solving activities.

Feedback Should Be as Psychologically Close to the Receiver as Possible

Psychological distance is a term used to indicate how involved and committed a person is to a source of information. The more involved and committed the person is to a source of information, the more likely he or she is to use the information to improve performance. Evaluators from outside the organization are psychologically more distant than someone from the personnel department who does a comparable evaluation. Outside systems also tend to be more technical and generalized, making it more likely that needed information may be left out and inappropriate information may be included. As a consequence, results fed back by someone in the organization will be more readily accepted than those fed back by an outsider. Similarly, an employee's immediate supervisor is psychologically closer than someone from the personnel department. The individual's own evaluation of his or her performance is psychologically the closest possible and thus is the most likely to affect the way he or she performs. In fact, self-assessment is so strongly believed that the individual will often ignore conflicting information from other sources.

Greller and Herold (1975) found that extrinsic (i.e., psychologically distant) feedback only had an effect on how much the employees liked the evaluator and not on any changes they made in their performance. When employees received positive information, they reported a positive orientation toward the evaluator. When they received negative information they were dissatisfied with the evaluator. Notice particularly that in neither situation were they dissatisfied with their performance and, as a consequence, had no impetus to change. They were dissatisfied with those who were telling them they performed poorly. The natural response was for them to increase the psychological distance between themselves and the offending source of feedback. Before individuals will be willing to pay attention to feedback they have to believe that it is accurate and the closer the source is to the individual psychologically, the more likely it is that he or she will perceive the information as accurate. The easiest feedback to believe is that which we give ourselves.

This creates an interesting question: What happens if we receive conflicting information about our performance? Two factors determine what kind of information will be believed and acted on. First is the kind of information provided; if it is positive and supporting, it is much more likely to be accepted than if it is negative. We like to hear good things about ourselves. The second factor is how much we identify with and respect the source of the information. Information provided by one's immediate supervisors is generally more readily believed than that of an unfamiliar personnel specialist. Because of these two factors, information we obtain ourselves is the most powerful form of feedback. If an external negative evaluation does not match our positive self-evaluation, we are very likely to ignore the outside information or even attack its source. Feedback systems should be developed that enable employees to obtain reliable, accurate information about their performance for themselves.

THE NATURE OF THE FEEDBACK SYSTEM: WHO GETS THE INFORMATION AND HOW IS IT PROVIDED?

Once we understand the characteristics of the information to be provided, we can design a system to generate the desired data. The nature of the data will determine how they are best collected.

Input information deals with available resources and is often best collected by management information systems that deal with data such as inventory levels, financial resources, production material and worker skills. It is "count data". Input resources are monitored by some established measurement system and reported in aggregate form to keep management informed of how many and what kinds of resources are available.

Process information is best collected by observations of people's behavior. It is information on how people relate together and what they do.

The best way to collect *output information* will be determined by the nature of the output; however, in all cases, it should be measured by comparison with the desired goal. Output data are often gathered through the use of physical measurements instead of the psychological and behavioral measures used for process data. This does not mean, however, that output data is any more valid than process data. Data that appears as dollars, tons, pieces, or minutes somehow seems to be more valid than measures of attitudes, interests, or skills; they aren't necessarily. For example, dollar values are built on a certain economic system and set of assumptions. Dollar values are determined by how the accounting system aggregates the information. Tremendous variation can result from different accounting systems. Dollars are a valid measure of worth only if you accept the assumptions of the accounting system that reports them. The problem with physical measurements such as dollars is that too often we accept them as accurate without questioning their underlying assumptions.

To summarize, the nature of the job should determine the nature of the feedback provided to the worker and how data are collected; they must be congruent. Do not focus on improving interpersonal skills by giving feedback on quantity produced or try to manage a cooperative situation using competitive data.

After developing feedback systems that provide the proper information, the next step is to implement the system by deciding who gets the information and how it should be provided.

Who Gets the Information?

The individuals responsible for actually doing the work should receive the information. They are ultimately responsible for meeting performance standards and only they can make the changes necessary to improve performance. The performer should receive the feedback directly; the more people the information is filtered through, the greater the chance personal bias will affect the accuracy of the information. If I receive feedback about your performance and am then responsible for transmitting it to you, naturally I will emphasize the information I think most important. If I am responsible for interpreting the data as well as transferring it to you, I am also likely to distort the information according to my own perceptions. All types of information are distorted when transmitted but especially process information (i.e., data that describes how a job is being done), because process information is not easily quantified.

Providing feedback directly to the performer also has other obvious advantages. Feedback reduces delay as much as possible; the performer receives the data as soon as they are available. The more people to whom the information is transmitted, the longer feedback will take. When information goes directly to performers, they can react quickly and deal with current problems.

How Should Feedback Information Be Provided?

For feedback to affect what performers are doing, it has to be used. Feedback will only be used if it is related to what the individual is trying to accomplish and is accepted as valid. Therefore, performers should be involved in developing the feedback system. Employees need to understand what is to be accomplished and have some say about the kind of feedback they receive. In fact, research suggests the best way to get people to use feedback information is to have them involved in developing the information and feedback system.

Because of this, make the feedback process part of the work itself. Individuals should be able to evaluate their own performance, then the feedback process becomes an intrinsic part of the job rather than something the individual receives from another person. One way to make feedback part of the work is to set concrete, measurable goals. Measurement of progress towards the goals can then be included in the work process.

For many jobs, feedback is an automatic outcome of the performance process. For example, computer programmers write programs to do certain computations. The programmers have not completed their job until the programs are submitted to the computer and run. Feedback on a computer programmer's accuracy is part of the performance process. Salespeople also receive feedback as part of their jobs; they either make a sale or they don't, and when they make one, they are the first to know about it. In both cases, the mere doing of the job provides the feedback: it is automatic and immediate.

Other types of jobs have feedback available but not as a natural result of the performance process. In fact if we want it, most of us have to build feedback into our jobs. Thus, one way of making feedback an intrinsic part of the performance process is to make evaluation one of the requirements of the work. Emery Air Freight provides a good example of how this is done. Their employees are required to evaluate their performance in relation to the preestablished goals. They do this by developing evaluation forms, checkoff systems, weighing devices, monitoring equipment, etc. that provide employees with feedback. For example, an employee might keep track of the volume and weight that is included in an air freight container. When the container is filled, the employee compares the total weight and volume against the goal to assess how well he or she has done.

Feedback should be made an integral part of the work process. Because most of us have jobs where feedback is not a natural part of the work process we need to make a conscious effort to include it in our work.

SUMMARY

Feedback is a crucial part of the performance process. Without it, management becomes an endless process of setting useless goals. When establishing a feedback system, four basic questions must be answered.

1. What types of information should be collected and reported? Information is available about what has happened at each stage of the performance process. The key is to feed back the information that will be most helpful to both employees and supervisors in managing performance.
2. How should the information be fed back to the employee? Should the employee's performance be compared to a goal, to his or her own past performance, or to the performance of others? It depends on what type of behavior you wish to encourage. Information concerning prior and present performance encourages people to maximize their own rewards. Information concerning one's own and others' performance encourages competition. Information concerning the group's present and prior performance encourages cooperation with those in the group. Information concerning another person's present and prior performance encourages focus on helping others.
3. What characteristics should the feedback have to be useful to those receiving it? No matter the type of information and how it is provided to employees, feedback should be descriptive, specific, directed towards factors the receiver can do something about, take into account the needs of both the giver and receiver, be appropriately timed, and psychologically close to the receiver.
4. Who should receive the feedback? The person doing the work.

TEN
MANAGING PERFORMANCE

Let us summarize what has been suggested in this book. The concepts are not particularly new but simply a way of thinking and managing that focuses on performance. The argument is that managers are responsible for performance so they should use it as the basis for what they do. First, managers should identify their goals, second, they should work towards accomplishing them, third, they should continually monitor progress, and fourth, they should adjust their strategy based on results. Performance is managed by managing these stages of performance.

Performance management can only flourish if certain conditions are met:

1. The organization must have the resources and flexibility to support a performance management system and must be able to change itself and its goals when necessary.
2. The employees must be concerned about performance. They have to be selected, trained, and managed based on their ability to contribute to organizational performance.
3. Managers must get their "kicks" out of seeing other people succeed. Management is "vicarious work." If managers don't learn this principle, instead of managing they will become deeply involved in doing the jobs they were hired to supervise. Employees will not be performing, and the unit will have lost a manager.

The performance management perspective can be applied to any of the activities involved in managing human resources. People can be recruited, hired, placed on jobs, trained, and transferred based on their performance or performance potential. Let us review the principles of performance management and how they can be applied using the Union Carbide Management System, which is much like other organizations' systems, as an example.

MANAGING THE PERFORMANCE PROCESS

Performance management is composed of two elements: performance and management. Performance can be broken down into five different stages.

Stage I:	Goals: Performance Expectations
Stage II:	Communicating Performance Expectations
Stage III:	Activities
Stage IV:	Results
Stage V:	Feedback

A complete performance management system will include all of the stages. For example, consider the Union Carbide Management System (see Figure 10-1). From the *Business Plan,* individual performance goals are developed consistent with the job responsibilities of the employee as described in his or her *Position Charter* (Stage I).

Measures of Performance describing in detail the standards that should be met by the end of the period are established and communicated (Stage II). These measures of performance become the basis for the manager and employee to work together through *Periodic Results Reviews* to accomplish the desired results (Stage III). The *Annual Performance Appraisal* is a formal opportunity to discuss results and prepare for the next cycle of the performance process (Stage IV and V). Taken together, the components of the Union Carbide Management System are an ongoing process for managing performance. Managers and employees work together managing the performance process to accomplish the desired results.

Performance management can affect what is accomplished by making changes at any stage. Remember the process is managed at Union Carbide as well as in any other organization; accomplishments are what happen as a result.

The appropriate strategy for managing the performance process is to spend time and energy where it will most contribute to achieving the desired results. Two dimensions help determine what is the appropriate focus. First is the ability of the individual. In some situations, individuals are asked to perform using abilities they already have. In others, they must learn new skills. In general the more the employees must learn, the more management should focus on the first stages of the performance process, that is, developing the right abilities and learning the proper processes. When employees lack skills, excessive pressure for output can only lead to frustration.

The second factor determining the focus of management is the nature of the job itself. If the job is complex, that is, relatively unpredictable, good performance will be determined by how well the employee can monitor the environment and quickly adjust to changes. Management should focus on

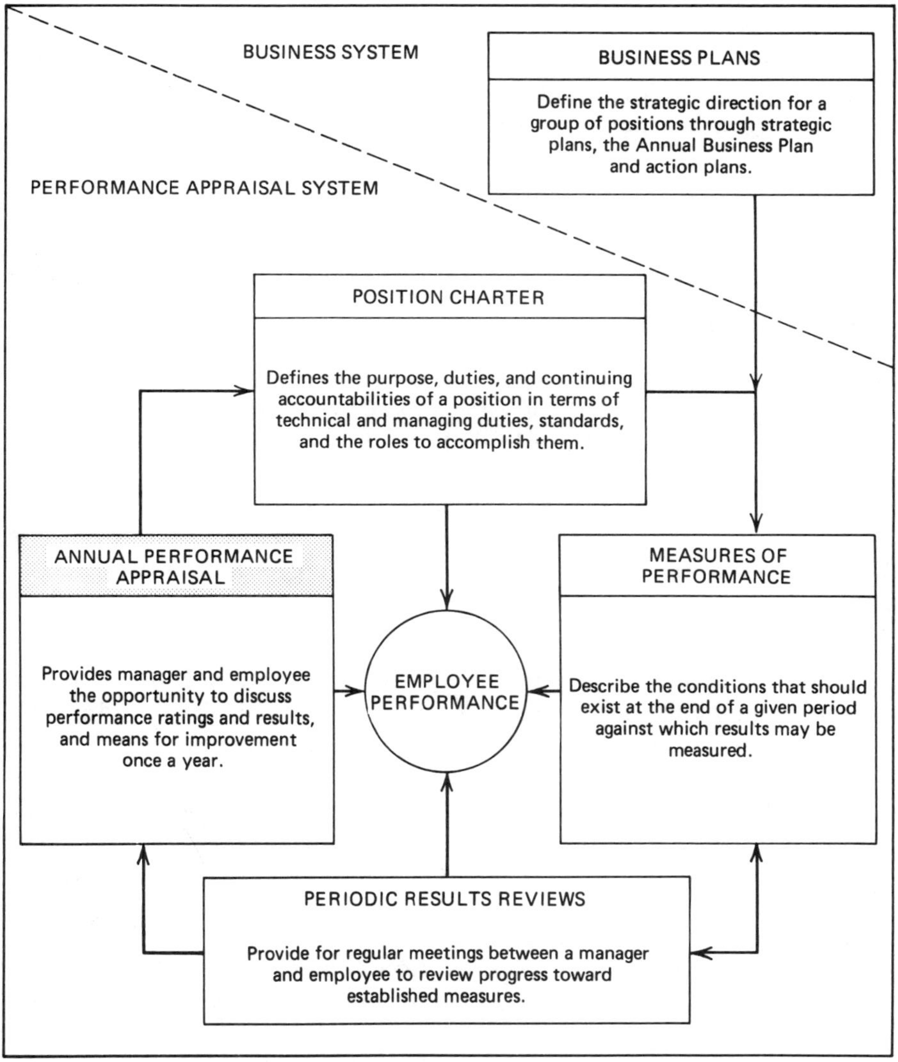

Figure 10-1 Union Carbide Management System. (*Source:* UCMS Annual Performance Appraisal, Union Carbide Corporation, 1983, p. 2.)

providing as accurate and complete information as possible and helping employees monitor and adjust to the environment, on the inputs and process of performance.

When the job is simple, that is, fairly predictable, management does not have to devote attention to monitoring the environment and making adjustments. Given realistic goals, the employees can manage the performance process themselves.

These two dimension can be combined to suggest the proper orientation when managing the performance process. In general, the simpler the job and the more highly skilled the individual, the more management should focus on actual results. The more complex the situation and the more the individual must learn the more the focus should be on what is used (skills and resources) and how the work is done (the process).

THE PERFORMANCE AUDIT

Performance does not happen in a vacuum, it happens in the context of an organization. The organization's technology and structure affect greatly what people do and accomplish. Only by understanding technology and structure can we properly manage human performance. The performance audit is a technique for assessing the contributions of technology, structure, and human resources to organizational performance. It identifies which of these factors is important, which is constraining organizational performance, and which ones you control. The performance audit has three steps:

1. Determine the contributing factors—the importance of the three general factors will vary depending on the nature of what is being produced. In service-oriented organizations, human resources will probably be the most important component; in advanced technology firms, the technology is most critical, and in complex problem-solving organizations, the relationship of the various specialities to each other (i.e., the organizational structure) often determines what will be accomplished.
2. Determine the constraining factors—even though a certain factor is the most important to the organization, it may not be the one limiting performance. For example, even if technology may be the most important factor in a certain business, lack of trained employees may be what is really limiting production. Employee training may make dramatic improvements in performance, even though technology is the most important factor.
3. Determine which factors you control—in the short run, you must focus on those factors under your control. For example, technology may be the most constraining factor in your firm, but if you don't control technology, you must accept it as a constraint to work with in the short run. Then, in the long run, you can try to gain more control.

The performance audit will identify how human resources fit within the organizational context created by technology and structure. It may tell you that the biggest impact on organizational productivity will come from changes in technology and structure. It may tell you that human resources are not the most important, but they are the factor constraining organizational performance. The performance audit will identify what is constraining organizational performance and what improvements to expect from changes in human resources.

Consider two units of Union Carbide as examples of different organizational contexts for managing performance. Both units use the same Union Carbide Management System but for each unit, the constraints and opportunities to manage human performance using the system are different.

The plants within the Chemicals Division produce chemicals used to manufacture a broad range of industrial products. The plants are very capital intensive and changes in technology are expensive and hard to make. The bulk of plant employees are material handlers and technicians who work with the machinery to control temperature and flows of material. The skills and effort needed from employees is dictated by the technology. Great improvements in human skills and effort beyond what is needed by the present technology will not have much of an impact until the technology is changed, but skills and effort below what is needed will destroy equipment and products.

Performance within the Controller's Group of the corporate financial organization at Union Carbide is managed within a far different context. The Controller's Group is responsible for all financial reporting and accounting of the corporation. Employees in the Controller's Group are accountants by training with experience in both managerial and financial accounting.

The accountants work with computers to collect and analyze data. The impact of more sophisticated computers will be limited by the skill and effort of the employees using them. Big improvements in performance come as employees improve their abilities.

In the Chemicals Division, human performance is critical to organizational performance but must fit within the technology. In the Controller's Group, human performance must also fit within but is much less constrained by the technology. In both units, the performance process is managed using the Union Carbide Management System. Even though the constraints are different types and degrees in each unit, performance is maximized when performance goals are set, activities managed, and evaluations done within the context established by the structure and technology. If the performance process does not fit the structure and technology, frustration will result. For example, if managers in the Chemicals Division develop employee performance expectations that cannot be accomplished because employees do not control the necessary technology or structure, the managers will be frustrated. If managers in the financial organization develop performance expectations that force employees unproductively to use outmoded technologies and structures, the employees will be frustrated.

THE IMPORTANCE OF ACCURATE STANDARDS AND MEASURES OF PERFORMANCE

Once management has decided where to focus attention, standards and measures of performance consistent with its focus must be developed. To do this, management must summarize the complex events occuring in the workplace. These summaries will usually involve numbers or descriptions of some sort. Whatever they are, they must be accurate in order to be useful. The accuracy of performance standards and measures can be determined by considering what is being measured, what the data mean, and how the data have been collected.

What Is Being Measured?

Whenever summaries are used, the question of whether they are truly accurate representations of the situation is raised. To develop accurate measures of performance the following steps must be taken.

1. Define the job.
2. Analyze the job to determine what the resources, skills, and activities and desired results are.
3. Develop standards of success.
4. Establish systems to measure progress against the standards.
5. Implement the system.

If unclear definitions of performance have been used to develop the performance standards and measures, you probably will not develop accurate measures. If you don't know what you are measuring, you can't measure it.

What Does the Measure Mean?

The meaning of data is determined by what is counted and how it has been summarized. A good way to consider what measures mean is to look at what has been counted and how.

How Are the Data Collected?

Measurement systems, whether they provide quantitative or qualitative data, must have certain basic characteristics in order to be accurate:

1. They must record both positive and negative aspects of performance.
2. They must be appropriately calibrated.
3. They should be taken as soon as possible after the performance they purport to measure has been completed.
4. They should be consistent.

If measurement systems have these characteristics, they will be accurate, usable summaries.

Organizations fail to develop accurate standards and measures for many reasons; they claim no one will use them, it takes too much time and money, and work is too subjective to be precisely measured. Compelling reasons, however, exist for developing accurate standards and measures. (1) Employees will focus time and efforts on whatever is defined as the standard, measured, and fed back. Consequently, the standards and measurement system will determine what employees do and accomplish. (2) The courts require that decisions affecting protected groups of employees be based on valid performance related criteria.

Developing accurate standards and measures costs both time and money and won't be worth the expense if they are not used. However, using invalid criteria doesn't save money; it just shifts the costs. Money may be saved initially because it is not spent on developing accurate measures, but much will be lost as bad decisions are made and opportunities lost.

MANAGING HUMAN RESOURCES

Within the context established by the performance audit, human performance is managed by doing the following:

1. Defining and communicating performance expectations.
2. Specifying and managing activities.
3. Controlling rewards the employee receives.
4. Managing feedback.

Each of these factors is reviewed below and explained using the development of a human resource information system for the controller's group at Union Carbide as an example.

Defining and Communicating Performance Expectations

Establishing performance expectations is a process of negotiation. Since employees receive information about what they are supposed to be doing on the job from many sources (superiors, peers, acquaintances, and the environment in general), they need some way to combine these expectations into a focused objective. A two-way discussion between employee and supervisor is the best way. The following six-step process is recommended.

1. Before the meeting, each party should develop a preliminary agenda including intial performance expectations to be discussed.
2. At the beginning of the discussion, the purpose of the interview should be discussed to determine if both parties agree on it.
3. After the purpose is clarified, the participants should agree on the way the discussion should proceed and what should be discussed.
4. During the discussion both participants should be actively involved. The supervisor should make sure the employee has a chance to air his or her opinions.
5. The supervisor should make sure that the discussion does not proceed to solving performance problems until both parties agree on what the problems are.
6. At the end of the discussion, conclusions should be summarized to make sure no differences or misunderstandings remain.

For example, the personnel manager for the financial organization at Union Carbide determined that performance would be substantially increased if managers had access to a human resource information system and the skills to use it. Working with a computer specialist, the personnel manager identified the type of system to develop and determined that such a system could be developed in five months. The computer specialist agreed to do the program and the personnel manager agreed to identify the data needed and the reports to be generated.

Specifying and Managing Activities

The first step in specifying and managing activities is to analyze present activities and how they might be changed to improve performance. Techniques for analyzing activities range from very objective time and motion studies to subjective interviews and questionnaires; both should be used if possible. Subjective measures will help you understand how employees view their work and thus how they are likely to act on the job; objective measures will help you understand the actual characteristics of the job so that you can consider what changes can be made.

If the analysis indicates that changes should be made, you can then determine which component of organizational performance—technology, structure, or human resources—can best be adjusted to improve the job. Your choice will be determined by which component you control. Changes in technology will have a direct and immediate affect on activities by determining what work needs doing and how it is to be done. Changes in structure will modify the employee's responsibilities and his or her relationships with others in the organization. Changes in human resources may involve hiring and firing or switching people into new jobs to bring in different skills and fresh ideas. Each component of organizational performance can be changed to affect employee activities. Any change you make to one component will affect the others, however, because they are all interrelated. For this reason, you have to consider all three components and their relationship to one another when you design or redesign the activities on a job.

For example, after the computer specialist began work developing the information system, the personnel manager analyzing the computer specialist job found that most of the specialist's time was spent programming the computer and little time was spent talking to managers who would eventually use the program. The computer specialist needed input from managers so he could develop a program that met their needs but his job was not structured so he had a natural way of receiving their help. Interviews were set up so the computer specialist could meet managers and a task force formed to help identify manager needs. The computer programmer's job was restructured to include both the interviews and meetings with the task force.

As the program was being developed, the personnel manager and the computer programmer meet weekly to review progress and redirect their efforts.

Controlling Rewards

Rewards are what people receive for performing. We assume employees value rewards and will do what is necessary to obtain them. Management can therefore improve performance by (1) defining what good performance is, (2) determining what the employee finds satisfying, (3) identifying the appropriate rewards, and (4) making the reward available when the employee performs well.

Organizations need various types of performance from their employees. They need them to become active members of the organization, they need them to do their job as it has been defined, and they need their employees to improve their performance. Each of these types of behavior can be motivated by different types of rewards. Systems rewards are automatically given to employees merely for being members of the organization. Individual rewards are given to employees based on the quality and quantity of their performance. Growth rewards are received by employees for job innovation, learning and improvement. The key to managing performance through rewards is to link the type of performance desired with the appropriate reward.

The following list gives some specific suggestions for managing performance through rewards.

1. Reward performance—if performance isn't being rewarded, something else is, something like group membership, who you know, luck, tenure, etc. The people receiving the rewards will be happy but the high performers won't.
2. Don't rely solely on the attitude surveys as the basis for management action. Knowing whether the level of employee satisfaction is high or low isn't enough. You have to know who is dissatisfied and why. The low performers should be dissatisfied and concerned about improving their performance so they can receive the rewards they desire and become more satisfied. If the high performers are dissatisfied, there are some real problems with your reward system.
3. Develop management support systems designed to assist individuals translate satisfaction and dissatisfaction into positive actions. You cannot assume dissatisfied employees will automatically work harder and try to do better. They may withdraw, do the minimum amount of work necessary to remain, leave the organization, or stay and sabotage it. Employees need clear responsibilities as well as training and counseling to help them understand how to meet performance requirements.

For example, the head of personnel for the Controller's Group is excellent using praise and recognition when working with others. The programmer was recognized as the developer of the human resource information system and involved in presenting it to management. The highlight of the development came in a management meeting when the programmer demonstrated the system. Management asked harder and harder questions. For each question, the programmer was able to call up the data and present the relevant report. Management became more and more enthusiastic and congratulated the programmer. The following performance appraisal the programmer success was appropriately reflected in his rating and compensation.

Managing Feedback

Feedback is what makes performance and management dynamic. Using feedback, actual results are compared to desired results as the basis for whatever adjustments need to be made. In this way, employees can learn from their past experience.

Different kinds of performance data will elicit different responses from employees.

1. Information about one's own performance—the employee will be concerned about maximizing his or her own accomplishments.
2. Information about one's own performance as compared to someone else's—the employee will try to outperform others with whom he or she is being compared.

3. Information concerning a group's performance—the employee will be concerned with maximizing the performance of the group of which he or she is a member.
4. Information concerning another person's performance—the employee will be concerned with maximizing another person's accomplishments.

The type of data you choose to give will be determined by what type of behaviors you want to elicit. In all cases, the characteristics of the feedback itself should be the same, that is, it should be descriptive, specific, appropriately timed, and directly related to the performance of the employee and appropriately timed.

For example, the programmer developing the human resource information system at Union Carbide received automatic descriptive, specific feedback each time he tried to make the system work. Unlike most people he worked with, the computer gave him error messages whenever mistakes were made. In their weekly meetings, the personnel manager also provided feedback on how the system being developed would meet the needs of management. The programmer was working toward his goal and received constant feedback from the computer and the personnel manager that he used to keep development on track.

DEVELOPING PERFORMANCE-BASED SYSTEMS

In summary then, performance is a process of accomplishing the desired results. Management is making sure that the correct things are accomplished. The performance process is not managed directly but is affected by the various systems in the organization. Who is placed on the job, how they are trained, the directions they receive, the rewards available, the relationships with other units, etc. all determine what is accomplished. Logically each of these decisions should be based on performance.

This book presented a general, performance-based approach that can be used to design any applied management system.

Step 1: *Define the performance process.* This will require an understanding of the ultimate objective and the stages work must go through. It is also important to recognize that situations change. Whatever definitions are developed must be flexible enough to accomodate the shifts necessary to remain effective.

Step 2: *Decide which stage(s) of the performance process, desired results, activities, actual outcomes, rewards, feedback are the most important at that particular point in time.* This decision will be determined by the competence of the individual and the complexity of the environment.

Step 3: *Complete a performance audit.* The performance audit is used to determine how technology, structure, and human resources relate to performance. It becomes the basis for making changes and improving performance. The main questions of the audit are: (1) What are the critical components of performance? (2) Which of the components do you control? (3) How should the components be changed to improve performance?

Step 4: *Develop accurate measures of performance.* Present conditions must be analyzed to determine what needs to be changed. Future potentials have to be described as concretely as possible so that appropriate systems can be designed. Both analyses and accurate descriptions require valid measures. Because measures are always summaries of the real world, there is the potential of missing important information. The measures should be as accurate a summary as possible.

Step 5: *Develop applied management programs consistent with the criteria and the factors that the performance audit identifies as being critical.* Particularly notice that this is the fifth step. It comes after a thorough analysis of the criteria and the constraints within which the manager must operate. Procedures and programs aren't appendages that hang on to an organization and become parasites. They have to contribute to the purpose of the organization. The best way to make sure this happens is to use the purposes of the organization as the basis for developing the program.

Step 6: *Continually evaluate the programs and procedures contributions to performance.* Just like everything else, administrative practices have to be evaluated for their contributions to performance. They can't develop a life of their own that goes beyond their usefulness. The only way to control the natural tendency to develop a vested interest in a certain way of doing things is to force self-evaluation to be an integral part of administrative practices.

Following these steps doesn't guarantee success. They do, however, provide a format for managing rather than just doing what comes naturally and hoping for the best. Approaching problems this way guarantees, at a bare minimum, that performance will be the beginning point of program development.

SUMMARY

Management is a complex and demanding profession because it is the manager who is responsible for making sure that the proper things are accomplished. It also can be tremendously rewarding when the desired results are reached. You can't win all the time and it's not easy. The best way to increase the probability of success is to use performance as the rationale for what is done. Natural human tendencies and organizational constraints are directly opposed to a focusing on performance. There is, however, one very compelling, overriding reason for doing it—performance!

REFERENCES

Adams, J. S. Toward an Understanding of Inequity, *Journal of Abnormal Social Psychology,* 1963, 67, 422–436.

Alderfer, C. P. An Empirical Test of a New Theory of Human Needs, *Organizational Behavior and Human Performance,* 1969, 4, 142–175.

Baird, L. S. and Hamner, C. Individual vs. Systems Rewards: Who's Dissatisfied, Why, and What Is Their Likely Response? *Academy of Management Journal,* 1979, 22, 783–792.

Baird, L. S. and Kim, J. Antecedents of Perceptions on Tasks, *Proceedings American Institute for Decision Sciences,* 1976, 165–167.

Baird, L. S. and Mainstone, I. Perceptions of Task Characteristics as Related to Job Involvement and Locus of Control, *Proceedings Northeast Aids,* 1975, 1–13.

Bales, R. F. *Interaction Process Analysis: A Method for the Study of Small Groups.* Cambridge, Mass.: Addison-Wesley, 1956.

Brief, A. P. and Aldag, R. J. *Task Design and Employee Motivation.* Glenview, Ill.: Scott, Foresman and Company, 1978.

Cascio, W. F. *Applied Psychology in Personnel Management.* Reston, Va.: Reston Publishing Company, Inc., 1980.

Charns, M. P. Individual and Organizational Correlates of Perceived Task and Environmental Characteristics, Working Paper, Carnegie-Mellon University Graduate School of Industrial Administration, 1976.

Fine, S. and Wiley, W. An Introduction to Functional Job Analysis, in E. Fleishman and A. Bass (eds.), *Studies in Personnel and Industrial Psychology,* 3rd ed. Homewood, Ill.: The Dorsey Press, 1974.

Frohman, A. *Critical Functions,* unpublished manuscript, Frohman Associates, Lexington, Mass., 1977.

Galbraith, J. and Cummings, L. I. An Empirical Investigation of the Motivation Determinants of Past Performance: Interactive Effects Between Instrumentality, Valence, Motivation, and Ability, *Organizational Behavior and Human Performance,* 1967, 237–257.

Gibb, J. Defensive Communication. *Journal of Communication,* 1961, 11, 141–148.

Goodman, P. S. and Friedman, A. An Examination of Quantity and Quality of Performance Under Conditions of Overpayment in Piece Rate, *Organizational Behavior and Human Performance,* 1969, 4, 365–374.

Greene, C. N. and Podsakoff, P. M. Effects of Removal of a Pay Incentive: A Field Experiment, Presentation at *Academy of Management National Meetings,* 1978.

Greller, M. M. and Herold, D. M. The Effects of Intrinsic and Extrinsic Feedback on Performance and Satisfaction, Working paper, New York University, 1975.

Guion, R. M. Criterion Measurement and Personnel Judgments. *Personnel Psychology,* 1961, 14, 141–149.

Hackman, J. R. and Oldham, G. R. "The Job Diagnostic Survey: An Instrument for the Diagnosis of Jobs and the Evaluation of Job Redesign Projects," *Technical Report No. 4,* Department of Administrative Sciences, Yale University, May 1974.

Hammer, W. C. and Harnett, D. L. Goal Setting, Performance and Satisfaction in an Interdependent Task, *Organizational Behavior and Human Performance,* 1974, 12, 217–230.

Hull, C. I. *Principles of Behavior.* New York: Appleton-Century-Crofts, 1943.

Kerr, S. On the Folly of Rewarding A. While Hoping for B. *Academy of Management Journal,* 1978, 18, 769–783.

Korman, A. K. *The Psychology of Motivation.* Englewood Cliffs, N.J.: Prentice-Hall, 1974.

Lawler, E. E. III and Suttle, J. L. A Casual Correlation Test of the Need Hierarchy Concept. *Organizational Behavior and Human Performance,* 1972, 7, 265–287.

Lewis, S. A. The Role of Perceived Competence, Outcome and Process Feedback in the Determination of Task Satisfaction. *Journal of Personality,* 1976, 44.

Locke, E. A. Toward a Theory of Task Motivation and Incentives. *Organizational Behavior and Human Performance,* 1968, 3, 157–189.

Luginbuhl, J. E. R., Crowe, D. H., and Kallan, J. P. Casual Attributions for Success and Failure, *Journal of Personality and Social Psychology,* 1975, 31, 86–93.

Maier, N. R. F., Haffman, L. R., Hoover, J. J., and Reed, W. H. *Superior-Subordinate Communication in Management.* New York: American Management Association, 1961.

McClelland, D. C. *The Achieving Society.* Princeton, N.J.: Van Nostrand, 1961.

McClintock, C. G. Social Motivation—A Set of Propositions, *Behavioral Science,* 1972, 17, 438–454.

McClintock, C. G. and McNeil, S. P. "Reward and Score Feedback as Determinants of Cooperative and Competitive Game Behavior," *Journal of Personality and Social Psychology,* 1966, 4, 606–613.

McCormick, E. J., Jeanneret, P. R., and Mecham, R. C. A Study of Job Characteristics as Based on the Position Analysis Questionnaire, Occupational Research Center, Purdue University, Report No. 6, 1969.

Maslow, A. H. A Theory of Human Motivation, *Psychological Review,* 1943, 50, 370–390.

Messick, D. M. and McClintock, C. G. Motivational Bases of Choice in Experimental Games, *Journal of Experimental Social Psychology,* 1968, 4, 1–25.

Murray, H. *Explorations in Personality.* New York: Oxford University Press, 1938.

Nadler, D. *Feedback and Organizational Development: Using Data-based Methods.* Reading, Mass.: Addison-Wesley Publishing Company, 1977.

Nagle, B. F. Criterion Development, *Personnel Psychology,* 1955, 6, 271–289.

Oberg, W. Make Performance Appraisal Relevant. *Harvard Business Review,* 1972, 50, 61–67.

Ordione, G. S. *Management and the Activity Trap.* New York: Harper & Row, Publishers, 1976.

Pepinsky, H. B. and Pepinsky, P. N. Organizations, Management Strategy, and Team Productivity, in L. Petrullo and B. M. Buss (eds.), *Leadership and Interpersonal Behavior.* New York: Holt Publishing, 1961.

Pfeffer, J. and Salancik, G. R. *The External Control of Organizations.* New York: Harper & Row, Publishers, 1978.

Porter, L. W. and Lawler, E. E. III. *Managerial Attitudes and Performance.* Homewood, Ill.: Irwin-Dorsey, 1968.

Rotter, J. B. Generalized Expectancies for Internal Versus External Control of Reinforcement, *Psychological Monograph.* 1966, 80.

Rummler, G. A. Human Performance Problems and Their Solutions, *Human Resource Management,* Winter 1972, 19, 2–10.

Skinner, B. F. *Contingencies of Reinforcement.* New York: Appleton-Century-Croft, 1969.

Smith, P. C. and Kendall, L. M. Retranslation of Expectations: An Approach to the Construction of Unambiguous Anchors for Ratings Scales, *Journal of Applied Psychology,* 1963, 47, 149–155.

Staw, B. M. Motivation in Organizations: Toward Synthesis and Redirection, in B. M. Staw and G. W. Salancik (eds.), *New Directions in Organizational Behavior.* Chicago, Ill.: St. Clair Press, 1977.

Thompson, J. D. *Organizations in Action.* New York: McGraw-Hill, 1967.

Toleman, E. C. *Purposive Behavior in Animals and Men.* New York: Century, 1932.

Tosi, H. and Carroll, S. *Management: Contingencies, Structure and Process,* 2nd ed. Chicago, Ill.: St. Clair Press, 1982.

Turner, A. N. and Lawrence, P. R. *Industrial Jobs and the Worker.* Boston, Mass.: Harvard University Press, 1965.

Vroom, V. H. *Work and Motivation.* New York: Wiley, 1964.

White, R. W. Motivation Reconsidered: The Concept of Competence, *Psychological Review,* 1959, 66, 297–333.

INDEX

Accurate measures, 56–60, 154–155
Activities, 5, 71–75, 96–118, 156–157
Analyzing jobs, 97–112
Attitudes, 128–131
Attitude surveys, 132–133

Behaviorally anchored rating scale, 50–52
Behavioral theories, 72–73

Cognitive theories, 73–75
Communicating performance expectations, 4–5
Competence of individuals, 13

Drive theory, 68–69
Dysfunctions of standards and measures, 62

Equity theory, 70–71
Expectancy theory, 73–75

Feedback, 6, 137–148, 158–159
  format for, 140–143
  management of, 158–159
  nature of system, 146–148
  useful characteristics of, 143–145
Feedback theory, 78–84
Functional job analysis, 101–106
Functional job attributes, 108

Goal theory, 67–68

Human resources, 25, 34, 115, 155

Information, types of, 137–139

Job analysis, 100–112
Job descriptions, 97, 98

Learning, 14

Management, 6–7
  of activities, 71, 96–118
  of information, 78
  of performance expectations, 67, 85–95
  of rewards, 75
Management by objectives, 9, 54

Need theory, 69–70

Objective data, 47
Organizational performance factors, 23–25

Perceptions, 98–99
Performance, 1–12
  components of, 30
  defining and measuring, 47
  dynamic nature of, 10
  process, 4
Performance audit, 23–45, 152–154
Performance based systems, 159–160
Performance expectations, 85–95
  establishing and communicating, 88, 155–156
Performance standards and measures, 46–66, 154–155
  accuracy of, 56–60
  activity standards and measures, 50–51
  developing, 60–62

Performance standards and measures (*Continued*)
  output standards and measures, 51–53
  predictive standards and measures, 49–50
Position analysis questionnaire, 107–108

Quantitative job analysis, 106–107

Reinforcement theory, 13, 72–73, 77–78, 119, 122–124
Reliability, 58
Results, 5–6
Rewards, 119–136, 157–158
  individual rewards, 122–124
  system rewards, 120–122
  tied to performance, 124–126

Structure, 25, 32–33, 114

Tasks, 15–21
Technology, 24, 31, 112–114
Time and motion studies, 100–101
Trait measures, 49

Validity, 56